CHARACTERS

CHARACTERS AROUND THE CROSS

Tom Houston

A ministry of World Vision

MARC
EUROPE

British Library Cataloguing in Publication Data

Houston, Tom
  Characters around the Cross.
  1. Jesus Christ—Crucifixion
  I. Title
  232.9'63   BT450

  ISBN 0–947697–21–7

MARC Europe is an integral part of World Vision, an international
Christian humanitarian organisation. MARC's object is to assist Christian leaders with factual information, surveys, management skills,
strategic planning and other tools for evangelism. MARC also publishes
and distributes related books on mission, church growth, management,
spiritual maturity and other topics.

Royalties accruing to the author from this book will go to the work of
World Vision.

DEDICATION

To Hazle, my wife, who has listened to all this
material and been a constant encouragement to me.

ACKNOWLEDGEMENTS

I acknowledge my debt to many books and commentaries over the years that have helped me to think of the Cross. I have not indicated sources in the text because the material has now become very much part of me and because they would disrupt the flow of the devotional narrative.

I have been grateful to my assistant Nathan Showalter and the staff of MARC Europe for their immense technical help in preparing the book and for their faith that it was worth doing. James Gibson has been particularly helpful in making the transition from the spoken to the written word.

I owe a great deal to many congregations and audiences in different parts of the world who have drawn this material out of me and listened appreciatively. Preaching is always two-way communication.

CONTENTS

PREFACE

Early in my Christian experience, I discovered that the Cross was—and needed to be—central in any understanding not only of the gospel, but of life itself. In the characters around the Cross we see the sins that brought Jesus there—the indifference of the crowd, the greed of Judas, the nepotism of Caiaphas, the envy of the chief priests, the neutrality of Pilate, the callousness of the soldiers—plain ordinary sins shown up for what they are against the backdrop of the Cross.

The longer I live the more I realise that the basis of life, as we experience it, is not rational, much as we would like it to be. Life is essentially tragic when it is lived by imperfect people in a fallen world. Only the Cross of Jesus can supply meaning in life when its basis is tragedy, and that is because the Cross was of a piece with the Resurrection that followed it. Jesus suffered the tragedy of the human condition and turned tragedy into hope; he returned from the dead to give men the second chance that never happens in tragedy. He rose from the dead to meet Mary Magdalene in the depths of her depression, to meet Thomas in his pessimism, to meet the travellers to Emmaus in their intellectualism, even to meet the chief priests in their frantic efforts to cover up the Resurrection.

My responsibility as a preacher has made it necessary for me to cover many times the accounts in the gospels of the suffering and death of Jesus. I have approached these stories from many different angles.

Perhaps the most fruitful angle has been the one re-flected in this book. I have tried to understand the characters of the main actors in this timeless drama. I feel I know them now and have to admit that as much of that knowledge comes from self-discovery as from the observation of others. So the pieces in this book are a mixture of my subjective reflection on the written text in the Bible. They cannot be de-finitive studies although I am deeply convinced of the truths they illustrate.

It has been impressed on me that perhaps the best commentary on the Ten Commandments is the Pas-sion and Death of Jesus. Apart from the command-ment about the worship of graven images, they all are broken or illustrated here. These have been soul-searching studies for me that have repeatedly 're-stored my soul'. I pray that they will do the same for every reader, as studies from previous generations have done for me.

CHAPTER 1

THE WAVERING CROWD

The prologue to the drama of the Cross, a scene devoted to the fickleness of the crowd, begins with the triumphal entry of Jesus into Jerusalem. At first glance it is a strange spectacle. On his way towards Jerusalem, Jesus sends two disciples ahead to Bethphage to commandeer a donkey. They return with an ass trailing its foal, and Jesus then adopts a means of transport—riding on an ass—that we never read of his using at any other time. He walked on all the other trips that he made that week; he seems even not to have used it on the return journey that day to Bethany.

Viewed from a modern perspective, however, the story is not so strange after all. It was a demonstration, deliberately planned and eminently successful. The time—Passover week—the place—the capital city of Jerusalem—and the method—dramatisation of prophecy—were all carefully worked out. The point of the demonstration was that Jesus was a king offering himself to the people. Zechariah had prophesied it: 'Rejoice, rejoice, people of Zion! Shout for joy, you people of Jerusalem! Look, your king is coming to you! He comes triumphant and victorious, but humble and riding on a

donkey—on a colt, the foal of a donkey' (Zech. 9:9,
GNB). Now Jesus was bringing it to life before their
eyes.

The people got the message and responded mag-
nificently. They laid their coats on the road as a car-
pet for him to ride over: a spontaneous red-carpet
treatment. They secured palm branches, the symbol
of victory, and both carpeted the road with them and
waved them jubilantly, enthusiastically in the air.
They chanted appropriate slogans: 'God save King
David's Son! God's man is here! Long live the King!'
By the time the demonstration reached the centre of
Jerusalem, the whole city was roused (Matt. 21:10);
and the crowd with Jesus at the front swept into the
temple area, through the bazaars of the sons of
Annas. There Jesus drove out all who bought and
sold, overturned the tables of the money-changers,
and drove out the animals. The authorities were furi-
ous, but the people were delighted. These ordinary
people had circumvented the system and successfully proclaimed Jesus their king; indeed it could not
have happened without them. The whole thing was
so popular with the crowd that the high priests were
powerless to do anything.

It seemed only a matter of time until Jesus took
over, but that never happened. Within five days the
same crowd was chanting very different slogans:
'Give us Barabbas! Away with Jesus! Crucify him!'
The crowd was so near rioting that Pilate could do
nothing except give the people their way. These ordinary people helped to put Jesus on the Cross;
again it could not have happened without them.

A Fickleness In People That Is Alarming

The fickleness of these ordinary people, seen in the drama of the Cross, certainly does not evoke admiration; yet this same fickleness of ordinary people-in-the-mass is endemic in human society.

Moses faced it. After the tremendous events of the Exodus, when the Children of Israel escaped from slavery in Egypt and crossed the Red Sea, the people seemed very committed to God and solemnly swore adherence to the covenant at Mount Sinai. In less than six weeks, however, they had swung around, persuaded Aaron to make them a golden calf to worship, and indulged in heathen orgies.

Joshua faced it. At the end of his life, when the people had possessed their new territory, he harangued them about their fickleness in turning en masse to the heathen practices of those they had driven out.

Elijah faced it. When Ahab and Jezebel called the tune and said that they should worship Baal, the people meekly left the faith of their fathers and complied. Elijah saw their superficiality and fickleness, for he asked, 'How long will you waver between two opinions? If the Lord is God, follow him; but if Baal is God, follow him' (I Kings 18:21).

We face it today. In the Third World, coups d'état and revolutions overthrow the established order. Often in a bloodless coup a few leaders are jailed while the mass of people meekly turn round and follow the new order. In our own society, people are no less wavering than the crowd in other countries. Clever advertising sends us into the streets, searching the shops for pet rocks or Cabbage Patch dolls or some other elusive source of happiness. The fine art of manipulation of the masses by the media sways our political opinions and leaves us vulnerable to the practitioners of mob control. Even in the Church, people are easily swayed by unscriptural ideas and cultic leaders. No crowd, not even our own, is immune. Only if we learn the secrets of steadfastness and stability in our outlook will be be safe from the swaying crowd.

If we examine the fickle Palm Sunday crowd there may be truths we can learn. Why did the people who were so keen on Jesus on Palm Sunday change so much that they helped to crucify him five days later on Good Friday?

Enthusiasms in People That Are Deceiving

The people's keenness on Jesus did not immediately wane after Palm Sunday. The reporters of that week take pains to point out that his popularity held out, perhaps even increased, right up until the Thursday. That popularity, however, was brittle, and when the mob manipulators got busy on the Thursday night and Friday morning, the people were swayed with relative ease. Some enthusiasms are not sufficient to promote stability in people.

Enthusiasms about past heroes

On the Monday of Holy Week the chief priests tried to trap Jesus by asking who had given him his authority. Jesus turned the question around and asked them from whom John the Baptist had received his authority, a clever answer because the crowd had definite opinions about John. The authorities were afraid of the people, for they all held that John was a prophet (Matt. 21:26). Luke even says that, if they denied John's authority, the crowd would stone them because they were persuaded that John was a prophet (Luke 20:6). Here then were people who had their history straight. They held right views about past events, but their right views about the past did not keep them from doing worse to Jesus than Herod had done to John.

It is easy to be wise after the event, and imagine that because we have a tidy view of the past, we are therefore ready for the present. Unfortunately it doesn't work that way. Just because we know the right does not guarantee that we will do the right. The Pharisees alleged that if they had lived in the days of their forefathers, they would not have taken part with them in shedding the blood of the prophets (Matt. 23:30). Jesus warned them that they were deceived and that their rewriting of history did not guarantee that they would not act in precisely the same way again. 'Go on,' he taunted them, 'finish up what your ancestors started.' And they did. Two or three days later, with the help of the wavering crowd, they had Jesus on the Cross. And like the Pharisees condemning their ancestors, we ourselves look at them and stoutly insist that if we had lived during Jesus' time we would have withstood the fickleness of the crowd. We very easily fall into the error that we are as good as what we know. A correct understanding of the past does not guarantee right action in the present.

Enthusiasm for exposing evil

Shortly afterwards, Jesus told the parable of the wicked husbandman and the vineyard, to show how people use what God entrusts to them for personal gain; not only do they make no return to God but are ready to defy God and even murder his Son. After he related the parable, 'The teachers of the law and the chief priests looked for a way to arrest him immediately, because they knew he had spoken this parable against them. But they were afraid of the people' (Luke 20:19). We can imagine the people having a big smile to themselves as Jesus so accurately exposed the greed and hypocrisy of their leaders. The people were not taken in. They seldom are. They knew what was going on. Yet the sequel shows that although they knew how self-seeking and unscrupulous their leaders were, this enthusiasm for exposing evil did not prevent them from turning and helping those same leaders to do the very evil in question. The people smiled on the Tuesday at the parable in which the tenants killed the owner's son so that the vineyard might be their own property; the same people on the Friday helped their leaders do that very thing. To know what is wrong and to enjoy seeing the evil exposed is not enough to guarantee that we ourselves will not be party to the same evil.

Enthusiasm for violent action

When the authorities were planning the arrest and execution of Jesus, they said, 'not during the Feast or there may be a riot among the people' (Matt. 26:5). The crowd seemed ready not only to stone the authorities if they insulted the memory of John the Baptist, but also to riot against their leaders if they touched Jesus. Such toughness and independence of judgement in the crowd should have made them keep their leadership in line, but it didn't work that way. A willingness to riot can easily be manipulated by an unscrupulous leader. After skilful agitation by the authorities the crowd threatened riot against Jesus for the chief priests; two days before, however, the chief priests had feared that the crowd would riot for Jesus against them. Willingness to use violence in one direction does not guarantee that a crowd will not turn round and use it for an opposite purpose.

Enthusiasm for Jesus as a teacher

Throughout that last week the Evangelists record again and again the crowd's enthusiasm for Jesus: 'The crowds answered, "This is Jesus, the prophet from Nazareth in Galilee"' (Matt. 21:11); 'the whole crowd was amazed at his teaching' (Mark 11:18); 'all the people hung on his words' (Luke 19:48); 'all the people came early in the morning to hear him at the temple' (Luke 21:38); 'the people held that he was a prophet' (Matt. 21:46); 'When the crowds heard this, they were astonished at his teaching' (Matt.

22:33); and 'The large crowd listened to him with delight' (Mark 12:37). It is quite a write-up. Their enthusiasm was certainly not in question, yet enthusiasm was not enough. Even after all that, they turned round and said, 'Crucify him!'

Nor will enthusiasm for Jesus as a teacher keep us from crucifying him in the twentieth century. Coming to hear his words and being astonished at his teaching are fine, but they are not enough. Admiring Jesus as a great teacher does not inspire devotion to the death, if necessary, for him or for the truth. Even knowing his teachings cannot provide an absolute guarantee against being manipulated to act against him. Jesus does not seek admiration and support from men. He had all the admiration and support one could ask for from the crowd; they got the point of his teaching; yet they still crucified him. Their acceptance of Jesus was superficial. What about ours? How deep does it go?

A Stabilising Commitment

Earlier in his life Jesus had put his finger on what was wrong with people. He said they were 'like sheep without a shepherd'. They did not belong to anybody. They had no one to guide them, protect them, or provide for them. In biblical language the word 'shepherd' was often applied to a king or princes or nobles to mean a leader. Prophets like Ezekiel and Zechariah complained that their shepherds fed themselves instead of their sheep. 'They are shepherds who lack understanding; they all turn to their own way, each seeks his own gain,' wrote Isaiah (Isa. 56:11). Jesus took up this prophetic refrain in his parable of the Good Shepherd, 'All who ever came before me were thieves and robbers ... he is a hired hand and cares nothing for the sheep' (John 10:8–13). Although the people had leaders, said Jesus, they did not have a shepherd. The crowd was left to stray, to go its own way, like sheep without a shepherd. What an accurate assessment! The crowd did not belong to anyone. They were on their own, able to be manipulated this way and that by the cunning of clever hirelings.

This brings us to the meaning of the Cross. Two things were happening at the same time: what men were doing and what God was doing. From man's viewpoint evil was overcoming good, but from God's viewpoint good was overcoming evil. Men crucified Jesus, but God 'laid on him the iniquity of us all' (Isa. 53:6). The Good Shepherd was giving his life for the sheep.

Jesus had recalled the prophecy as he left the upper room, 'It is written: "I will strike the shepherd, and the sheep of the flock will be scattered"' (Matt. 26:31). This was true leadership, leadership that recognised the sinful heart of man as the problem and took the most drastic measures to rectify the problem at its core. He suffered the consequences of our fickleness. He bore our sins in his body on the tree. He died, the reliable for the unreliable, the righteous for the unrighteous, so that he might bring us to God. The people were fickle and their crime was heinous, yet the grace of God was working in their fickleness. The death that they caused, because it was the death of the Son of God, atoned for their sins and for the sins of all men for all time. To the fickle crowd and to all men who have crucified him since, Jesus offers forgiveness and a new life if they will submit themselves to the dynamic, caring leadership of the Good Shepherd.

One last look at the Jerusalem crowd fifty days later shows the difference that the Cross made to the fickleness of the wavering crowd. In his sermon on the day of Pentecost Peter made the same point about the dual action at the Cross. 'This man was handed over to you by God's set purpose and fore-knowledge; and you, with the help of wicked men, put him to death by nailing him to the cross. But God raised him from the dead' (Acts 2:23, 24). The crowd was doing evil, but God was turning evil into good, offering forgiveness and new leadership to a leaderless people. The crowd, cut to the heart to hear it, asked what they should do. Peter told them to re-pent, be baptised, and receive the gift of the Holy Spirit. Three thousand of them did so in the days that followed, and the Church was born—a group of men and women whom authorities could no longer intimidate nor manipulate. 'We must obey God rather than men,' they cried, even in court. Neither prison, nor poverty, nor death held any terror for them, and they began to turn the world upside down. What a difference! Where did they lose their wavering? What was the secret of their steadfast-ness? It was that they responded to the love of God seen in the Cross, became completely committed to Jesus Christ, and were changed by God's Spirit within them. They had found the Shepherd. The

Shepherd had found them.

What about us? Ambivalent? Tossed this way and that? Up and down? Hot and cold? Once constant but now drifting? Do we belong to the wavering crowd that is sometimes for Christ and sometimes against him? Do we admire him as a great teacher, even support him occasionally with enthusiasm, but turn round and go with the rest when the pressure or the inclination in another direction is strong? The Cross of Jesus shows where that attitude can lead. Jesus is crucified afresh in every injustice done, in every liberty or right withdrawn, in every truth suppressed, in every victim sacrificed, in every person put to the wall, in every needy person neglected, in every case of discrimination. The wavering crowd crucifies him afresh in the twentieth century, but it can be different. The risen Christ offers himself as the Shepherd for the shepherdless, offers stability for fickleness, and the power to transform the wavering crowd into men and women completely committed to him.

CHAPTER 2

THE MATERIALISM OF JUDAS

The first scene in the drama, setting the stage for the conflict to follow, is played by my friend Judas. Why do I call Judas my friend? Because Jesus did. More than once the word that Jesus uses for Judas is *philos* or 'friend', quite a strong word in the original. I also call him friend because making friends with Judas helps us to understand ourselves. A television programme called 'A Face for Judas' was shown in Britain in the 1960s. It approached the subject by taking a television producer who had a programme to produce about Judas. He searched everywhere for the right person with the right appearance and the right characteristics to give him an idea of who Judas would be today. After he had searched in all directions, the television programme ended with a powerful shot of the producer looking into the mirror and saying, 'You'll do.' There is something of us in Judas, and there is something of Judas in us. We don't help ourselves when we put Judas over there with horror and us in imagined superiority over here.

Judas' Motive

So let's look at this man. There have been many

theories and guesses about Judas Iscariot—he was a nationalist, a disillusioned zealot, and so on—but there is absolutely no subtlety in the New Testament treatment of Judas Iscariot. Only one motive consistently explains his betrayal of Jesus. Money. He had the bag and took money out of it (John 12:6); he led the attack on Mary when she anointed Jesus' feet with the expensive perfume (John 12:4); he was given a bribe of thirty pieces of silver to betray Jesus (Matt. 26:15); and when his conscience bothered him, he thought mainly about returning the money (Matt. 27:3, 4). All this adds up to a consistent picture of materialistic motivation. He was a friend of Jesus to whom money mattered too much. As the materialist of the New Testament, Judas is a lesson to us all, for it was the materialism of one of his friends that crucified Jesus. The Cross shows us what materialism does.

This approach may seem to scale down the enormity of what Judas did—and rightly so, for most of us have problems understanding Judas. Was Judas fated to do what he did? Was his betrayal predestined? Can we condemn him if he had no choice in the matter? Yet, if we don't condemn him, we exonerate the most famous criminal of human history. When I was a young man, for example, I went to preach in the open air at a place called the Mound in Edinburgh, where speakers get heckled. I was a budding young preacher, trembling and shaking on the stand, and a man came up and heckled me, 'What about Judas?' And I said, 'What about Judas?' He said, 'Judas was a hero. His name should be blazoned above the shops there on Princes Street.' I

said, 'Why?' He said, 'He fulfilled his destiny. He
was a hero.'

This question of fatalism or determinism, however, becomes important only when Judas' act is
singled out as the evil of all evils. This the New Testament emphatically does not do. It was not the evil
of all evils; it was an ordinary course of evil shown
up for what it really was by being placed in the light
of Jesus Christ and of his Cross. That's where the
enormity comes. It was inevitable in the nature of
things that Jesus should be betrayed and that someone should do it, for this is what evil does when good
gets in the way. It was not inevitable that it should be
Judas in particular. He is not especially diabolical,
just one of a kind. The message is that all those like
him are as diabolical as he is—as diabolical as he is
seen in the light of the Cross.

To bear out what I say, let me mention three
things you may not have noticed. Apart from the
gospels only one other reference to Judas can be
found in the New Testament; it appears in Acts 1,
where his replacement is found and his place is filled.
There is only one reference after that in the New
Testament to the betrayal of Jesus, and it comes in
the institution of the Lord's Supper 'in the night in
which he was betrayed'. There Judas' name is not
mentioned. His act, not his person, is recalled. Apart
from that, apart from the gospel passages in
Matthew, Mark, Luke and John, there is no further
reference to Judas.

The second thing is that the Greek word translated 'betray' just means 'hand over'; it is translated
'betray' only when it is used of Judas. This is an

English aberration that sets out the word 'betray' as appropriate to Judas, when all the rest of the time that the Greek word is used (and it is quite frequent in the New Testament) it is not translated as 'betray' but as 'hand over.'

The third thing is that Judas is called 'one of the Twelve'. Now it may interest you to know that that phrase is used of only one other person only one other time. It is used of Thomas once in John 20:24. None of the rest is spoken of as 'one of the Twelve'. Of course, the Twelve are spoken about many times, but ten times Judas comes into the narrative of the gospels as 'one of the Twelve'. Look at it mathematically. The Twelve were the inner circle. 'One of the Twelve' means that eight and a half per cent of the inner circle betrayed Jesus, was guilty of this materialism. Could we not look at this as a likely proportion of the disciples affected seriously by materialistic considerations? One in twelve. Ten in one hundred and twenty. The proportion would be greater in the fringe of the Church. The proportion would be greater still outside the Church. But if we just think about 'one of the Twelve' mathematically, we are saying that in that proportion materialism is to be found in the inner circle of Jesus' friends. And that is enough, surely, for us to be asking, 'Lord, is it I?' Or to be asked, 'Friend, why are you here?'

Materialism: anxiety for lack of money or things; the effort to get money or things; the compulsion to hoard; meanness; carelessness; the compulsion to spend. It's an ugly picture. In our own friendship with Jesus, do we ever betray Jesus Christ for materialistic considerations? To answer this, let us look at one or two statements about Judas that will light up the subject.

Materialism Is Secretive

It is known to Jesus, but not known to others. Has it ever struck you that the disciples were completely and utterly taken by surprise at what Judas did? When Jesus assumed that one would betray him, as we read in the passage, the disciples looked at one another, uncertain of whom he spoke. No one at the table knew why he said this to Judas. It was only afterwards that they knew. They didn't know about his pilfering the petty cash. They didn't know that he had been to the authorities. Among them, yet not known to them, he was able to masquerade as one of them. Their friends were his friends, while all the time personal gain controlled him. Judas completely deceived the eleven by his friendliness. He pretended to be a disciple when he was a devil, to think of the poor when he cared not for the poor, to be interested in economy when his interest was in dishonesty, to be ignorant—'Lord, is it I?'—when he had already made the pact with the authorities. He pretended to be intimate with Jesus, taking the sop from him as the privileged gesture at the meal, while in fact, in mind, and in intention he was already the betrayer. He had the behaviour of a saint but the heart of a miser.

Materialism is always hidden, secretive. Francis Xavier, the great Roman Catholic priest, said that in the confessional men had confessed to him all the

sins that he knew and some that he had never imagined, but that none of his own accord confessed
that he was covetous. If materialism, dishonesty, is
in us, there is a chance that it is known only to ourselves and to God. Yet the fact that it is not known
does not mean that it is not ruinous, and we need to
search our hearts and be honest. It was about money
that Jesus said, 'If then the light within you is darkness, how great is that darkness!' (Matt. 6:23). That
was a statement about finance, about self-deception
concerning materialism. And we could add here in
Judas' case, 'If the friendship that is in you is false,
how false is that friendship!' There are many
friendships where the underlying motive is greed,
and the friendship is false.

Materialism Rationalises

We always look for ways to explain our greed, but
Jesus is not taken in. To rationalise is to find good
reasons for what you want to do anyway. We see
this in Judas in the case when Mary anointed Jesus
with her expensive perfume. Judas wanted this kind
of money to go through his bag so that he could take
his rake-off. If there was to be generosity like that,
Judas approved it as long as the money was put
through the general fund so that he could control
what happened to it in his own interests. It was as
simple as that, but it was not presented as that. It was
presented as depriving poor people of what they
might otherwise have. 'Why wasn't this perfume
sold and the money given to the poor? It was worth

a year's wages' (John 12:5). A very worthy senti-
ment. Or again it was presented as waste. 'Why this
waste?' says Matthew. Certainly, it is also a worthy
practice to avoid waste. Jesus had said so when he
ordered the fragments to be gathered up after feeding the five thousand. Judas' argument was plausible
and carried the others along with it.

So this is how materialistic motivation works: it
always has a few good reasons handy to justify what
we want to do anyway. We have our families to
think of; we must lay up for a rainy day; we need to
keep up our status; people must be taught to work
for anything they get... Hence we're not to imagine
that when Judas decided to hand Jesus over to the
authorities, he necessarily saw it as betrayal at all.
It's more than likely, especially with the sequence of
events, that he had what seemed like good reasons
for doing what he did.

One widely argued theory is that Judas went to the
authorities in order to force Jesus' hand, to make him
use his power to have himself installed as king. When
it didn't work out that way, he was upset and tried to
undo the damage. Not the slightest shred of evidence
in the New Testament supports that theory, but it
does show that Judas would have rationalised what he
did to such an extent that it seemed that there was jus-
tification for doing it. If we examine ourselves to detect materialistic motivation, we must not look for
blatant greed in ourselves. We must look at some of
the apparently good or wise things we do or say and
penetrate through them to their materialistic heart as
Jesus did when he looked at Judas. He knew what this
man was like, though nobody else did.

Materialism Defiles

When Jesus wants to cleanse, materialism keeps us dirty. 'And you are clean, though not every one of you,' he said to them when he was washing their feet. 'For he knew who was going to betray him, and that was why he said not every one was clean' (John 13:10, 11). When Jesus comes into any of our gatherings, if there is materialism there, he has to say, 'You are not all clean.' Outward washing does nothing, unless the heart or inner personality is cleansed, and that cannot be cleansed as long as it is gripped by covetousness. Jesus had already said the same thing through other pictures. Treasures on earth become the moth and rust that corrupt the heart that cherishes them. In the same passage in the Sermon on the Mount he says that money or materialism brings darkness to a man's soul. One of the things that makes me shudder, and always has, is that what we do with money does something to us. Every penny we get and every penny we spend does something to us. It corrupts us or ennobles us.

Materialism Enslaves

Luke and John both tell us that when Judas decided to hand Jesus over, Satan entered into him so that his action was well-nigh inevitable. Now this is true to character not only of greed but also of sin in general. The more often we commit sins, the stronger hold they have over us. Jesus compares this to slavery. Do you remember the Sermon on the Mount? You can't serve God and money—Mammon. Why? It's impossible because of the hold that each maintains over you. As materialism advances, as materialism becomes more important than other considerations, more important than *any* other consideration—we imagine that we will work or we will cheat until we have made enough money or until we have built up some security. Then, we imagine, things will be different. Then we can relax and give time to other things. It doesn't happen. What's the most addictive thing in life? Is it alcohol? Is it drugs? I don't believe so. The most addictive thing in life is money. It enslaves and we don't see it. It works like a drug. We get hooked, and there is never a time when we don't want more.

Materialism Twists Values

Materialism also warps values. Jesus gives us the right values. Thirty pieces of silver—unfortunately, we don't quite know what those 30 pieces of silver were valued at. There are two possibilities. If they were shekels, they would be the equivalent of about 120 days' wages. If they were denarii, they would be the equivalent of 30 days' wages for a soldier or a working man. So there are the two ends—at the most 120 days' wages, at the least 30. Whatever it was, Jesus was worth less to Judas than those 30 pieces of silver. Compare, on the other hand, the expense of perfume worth 300 denarii, a year's wages for a working man, that Mary spent in one loving act just to honour and please her friend. That loving act

Jesus commended, but to Judas money and getting on were more important than people. He was ready to sacrifice the innocent, even his friend, to get where he wanted. What about us? What about our values? Where do people and money fit in? We may not be ready to betray our best friends for 30 pieces of silver, but whom else and what else might we be willing to sacrifice if the price were right? The warping of our values happens so imperceptibly that we do not realise how like Judas we have become.

There is an interesting story behind Leonardo da Vinci's painting of the Last Supper. The artist had finished painting everyone except Judas, and he needed a model for that person. He went out and looked in all the bad places of the city, and at last after some years he found a man who was a type of the world's derelicts. On his face was stamped the effect of sin; guilt and remorse seemed written all over it. Furtive eyes and shifty gaze spoke of a life of deception and fraud. The artist thought, 'There's my man.' So he asked him to come to his studio. When the man came in, he glanced around. The place looked familiar to him. 'I have been here before,' he said. 'My God! I am the man that you painted for Christ some years ago; now you've taken me for Judas. Is that all I'm fit for? Is that what I've come to?' Warping of values takes place slowly.

Materialism and Judas

What made Judas do it? We don't know. There is one fact, however, that even if not true of him, has been true of others, in similar situations. The name 'Iscariot' might mean 'Ish-Kerioth' or 'a man of Kerioth', making Judas the only non-Galilean in the Twelve. Was Judas made to feel the odd man out, and was money his way of getting his own back or compensating by raising himself in his own and others' eyes? Was it reaction to the fact that he felt different that he had to over-compensate by getting on materially? We don't know. We do know that a feeling of non-acceptance has done this in other men and women, perhaps even in some of us. There are some who compensate for a sense of inferiority in one respect by the display that they can put on with their clothes or their home or their car.

The picture of Judas, however, although terribly sad, is not wholly black. He saw his sin. His conscience was not completely insensitive, and when it gave him no rest, he tried to do something about it. He tried to get out. He went back. He admitted his sin. 'I have sinned,' he said, 'for I have betrayed innocent blood' (Matt. 27:4). But he found a stony response. It is always difficult to get out of a bribe, for there are two parties involved. The confession of one is a threat to the other. That's why Isaiah says, 'whoever shuns evil becomes a prey' (Isa. 59:15). He exposes himself to be devoured by others. There are men both in private and public life who, if they followed their consciences, would resign. They have often thought about it, but if they were to move, they would involve other people. It is very difficult. Some of them are worse than Judas: they still have the money; they are still in the position and have the favour that goes with it. Judas did two tremendous things: he admitted his crime and he returned the money. Although the authorities would not co-operate and take it, he would not keep it. Instead, he threw it down and went away and took his own life. Tragic.

This need never have happened. Jesus did everything to draw Judas the other way—called him 'friend' and he meant it, made him one of the Twelve, called him 'chosen' although he knew what he was capable of from the beginning, gave him responsibility, made him treasurer of the party. What would we have done? Set up an audit system to make sure that money couldn't be taken out of the bag? Jesus trusted this man with the money although he knew what was in him. Jesus washed his feet as he washed the others' feet; he gave him the place of honour on his left in the Last Supper and gave him the morsel as an indication of friendship. All the time he was trying to draw this man Judas. 'Come out of where you are and come to me. Judas, my friend, I love you. I accept you. You can be different'. Instead, Judas went out into the night of his own making, a night of loneliness and isolation. The tragedy is that Judas never saw the Cross. He only heard that it was going to take place and did not think it was a good idea. He didn't see it; he didn't understand it; and he took his own life before he knew about the atonement. What a tragedy! The dying thief on the cross—just as bad as Judas—heard Jesus say, 'Today you will be with me in paradise.' Peter after the Cross—just as bad as Judas—heard Jesus say, 'Peter, do you love me? Feed my sheep.' But this man Judas took his life before the Cross was enacted, before he understood its meaning, and died in isolation and remorse.

We see in the Cross, then, what materialism did in one out of 12 of Jesus' friends. The man who could come and kiss Jesus and be expected to do so was the one who handed him over. What about us? What about the Christian Church represented by us? How materialistic is the Church?

I suppose that the answer to that has to be that the Church is as materialistic as the sum of materialism in its members. And if we are materialistic, do we hinder the purposes of God in his Church? I'm sure that we do. So we need to ask ourselves that question of our friend Judas, 'Lord, is it I?' Jesus was wounded in the house of his materialistic friends, but Jesus died for Judas his friend, for all the eight and a half per cent in the inner circle of his disciples, his friends, and the greater number of fringe folk who see themselves in him. And to know forgiveness, we need to add one thing that Judas did not. He confessed, he restored, but he never came to believe and accept forgiveness and the reconciliation that forgiveness brings. Let us pray that we may.

CHAPTER 3

THE NEPOTISM OF CAIAPHAS

The principal actor in the trial of Jesus, both behind the scenes and on centre stage, was the high priest Caiaphas. His sin was nepotism.

The word 'nepotism' comes from the Latin *nepotes* which means 'nephews'. It arose in the Middle Ages when it was applied to the so-called 'nephews' of the Pope, his illegitimate children who were given honours in public life. Eventually 'nepotism' came to mean favouritism in public life towards relatives, and it has featured in the public life of every country. In Swahili they talk about 'brotherisation,' and that is nepotism.

The book *Corruption in Developing Countries* by Wraithe and Simpkins, points the finger even at Britain:

> British institutions work manifestly for the advantage of certain people and quite as clearly do not benefit others. Why, for example, are thirteen of our prime ministers and roughly the same number of foreign secretaries and chancellors descended from Sir George Villiers, an Elizabethan squire? Why are so many

cabinet ministers, bishops, judges, and top managers drawn from such a small group of public schools? In the time of Walpole, not long after the Scottish Lord Bute became Prime Minister, there were sixty-three Macs, twenty-five Campbells, an uncertain number of Hamiltons, and many others of Scottish descent to be found on the pensions list.

Nepotism exists not only in Third World countries today, but is part of the life in every country.

Nepotism does have a right side to it. It has a very natural origin. Caring for your own kith and kin is natural. Blood is thicker than water. Paul says to Timothy, 'If anyone does not provide for his relatives, and especially for his immediate family, he has denied the faith and is worse than an unbeliever' (I Tim. 5:8). We are set in families by God for the specific purpose of helping each other, and everyone has a duty out of his own means to provide for his relatives and to help them as he is able. The trouble with nepotism begins when one uses public office or public funds or one's employer's means to help relatives who may not be at all as destitute as those to whom Paul refers. Nepotism is especially wrong when partiality to one's family or one's clan or one's tribe excludes others of more competence and greater ability. The question to ask, then, is whether nepotism is good or bad, and if bad, whether or not it will be tolerated. For the answer we must look at the life of Jesus Christ and especially at the Cross and the part played by Caiaphas, the high priest and prime mover in the conspiracy to have Jesus put away.

The Family of Annas

To begin with, let us look at the history of nepotism in the family of Caiaphas. John's account of the arrest of Jesus mentions Caiaphas and his father-in-law Annas. 'Then the detachment of soldiers with its commander and the Jewish officials arrested Jesus. They bound him and brought him first to Annas, who was the father-in-law of Caiaphas, the high priest that year' (John 18:12, 13). This old man Annas is the person to concentrate on. He appears again in a rather strange sentence in Acts 4:6 when the Sadducees are acting against the early Christians for preaching the Resurrection. 'Annas the high priest was there, and so were Caiaphas, John, Alexander and the other men of the high priest's family.'

Here Annas is called the high priest, and when the Jewish leaders wanted to act, they had to consult that family. The explanation is this. The office of the high priest was at the disposal of the Roman procurator. Annas was appointed by Corillius in AD 7. He lasted for seven years and was then put down by the next man called Valerius Gratus, who came from Rome. But Annas wasn't easily pushed aside, and this same Valerius Gratus was dancing to his tune again two years later, when he appointed Annas' son Eleazer to this highest Jewish political office.

Apparently, Eleazer did not please the Romans,

and a year later he was deposed. But Annas' family made a comeback. After another year when the replacement was deposed, Caiaphas, Annas' son-in-law was appointed. He is our man. And it seems that the tussle with the Romans was won by him, for he lasted 18 years until AD 36. He was in office when Pilate came to be governor; we can see from the gospels how well he managed him. But even that wasn't the end of the story; after Caiaphas, four more sons of Annas were made high priests: Jonathan and Theophilus both in AD 36 (in quick succession), Matthias in AD 42–43, and Annas the Younger in AD 63.

What a powerful family they were! As the Roman governors pushed them out, the family got together and schemed until they had another member of the family in. The brain behind it was the old man Annas. He did rather well. With himself and five sons and one son-in-law in the office, he dominated Jewish political life for half a century.

According to Matthew's account even the meetings of the council took place in the high priest's house. It was just about this time, 40 years before the destruction of the temple, that this Jewish Sanhedrin or parliament or council moved from its traditional meeting place in the chamber of hewn stone to the bazaars, the house of the high priest. This is further evidence that the council was in the pocket of this man. If Caiaphas were alive in Britain today, he would be regarded as a highly successful and astute person. Josephus, the Jewish historian, put it like this:

They say that this elder was most fortunate for he had five sons, and it happened that they all held the office of high priest to God, and he himself had enjoyed that dignity a long time before. This had never happened to any other of our high priests.

So what was the secret of this man's power? of this family's power? There is little doubt that it was their wealth. Josephus says that Annas was a great hoarder of money. Naturally, as high priests the family had control of the temple, and even when the temple affairs were conducted honestly, that meant a considerable income from the temple tax and from the sacrifices that they were allowed to take for themselves and consume or sell. Jim Bishop in *The Day Christ Died* (1957) gives a figure for the high priest's income, and I have tried to compute it up to date. I wouldn't be far out if I said that from the temple tax and the sacrifices the high priest enjoyed an income of £3.5 million per annum. But that wasn't enough. This astute family dreamed up other lucrative sources of income. The money changers, as Edersheim in *The Life and Times of Jesus* calculates, received about 12½ per cent of the change of funds; that would come somewhere in the region of £2 million. Then there were inspection charges—about £3.50 per animal. In the bazaars of the sons of Annas, as they were called, there were the sales of animals for the folk who couldn't bring an animal. The temple market and the bazaars of the sons of Annas are identical, says Edderscheim. At the feast times the prices were probably approximately the equivalent of £17.60 for two pigeons. One one occasion before the great Hillel, they were reduced before night to about two per cent of that. It was a tremendous racket! Not surprisingly, the people detested the sons of Annas. The Talmud, that great Jewish book, even records a curse on them. 'Woe to the sons of Annas, themselves high priests, their sons treasurers, their sons-in-law assistant treasurers, while their servants beat the people with sticks.' This harsh picture paints the background for the trial and death of Jesus. It's not a pretty picture, but some things become much clearer when we know about the family.

Nepotism Is Short-sighted

The first encounter between Jesus and Caiaphas shows that nepotism, or over-concentration on family to the detriment of others, is short-sighted. It is a here-and-now outlook. The council of elders was called because many people, too many people, were believing in Jesus. They were afraid that it would lead to insurrection and intervention on the part of the Romans, who would take away their place and nation. Caiaphas joined the debate and said, 'You know nothing at all! You do not realise that it is better for you that one man die for the people than that the whole nation perish ... So from that day on they plotted to take his life' (John 11:49–53). The issue here was their view of the Resurrection. Many times in the New Testament, soon after the event of a

resurrection or any mention of it, the Sadducees—
and Caiaphas was a Sadducee—were there and ac-
tive. The Sadducees didn't believe in the Resurrection, and they sprang into action whenever resurrection was talked about or experienced. The raising of
Lazarus from the dead, for example, prompted them
into action. It wasn't just that people were believing
in Jesus; it was that resurrection was a possibility.
The only question to Jesus during Passion Week by
the Sadducees was about resurrection. 'Do you remember the woman who had been widowed seven
times? Whose wife was she?' That was a Sadducee
question. Their view was that there was no afterlife,
so she couldn't belong to anybody. Jesus's answer
was that family connections don't carry over in the
same way in the resurrection. There would be no
marrying or giving in marriage, he said, but there is
a resurrection.

Even after the Crucifixion, when they were seal-
ing the stone, the Sadducees and the chief priests
were worried about resurrection. They gave money
to the authorities and said, 'So give order for the
tomb to be made secure until the third day. Otherwise, his disciples may come and steal the body and
tell the people that he has been raised from the dead.'
And then the sentence—'This *last deception* will be
worse than the first' (Matt. 27:64). What was this *last
deception*, the *last lie*? The Resurrection! The last lie
was not a lie, but it was fatal to the Sadducees' creed
and to their practice of nepotism if the truth of the
Resurrection could be established.

If you bring the Resurrection and afterlife into
view, it makes nepotism or all this concentration on

family just so much folly. Jesus illustrates it in the
contrasting cases of the rich man and the other
Lazarus. In the afterlife the rich man wanted to send
somebody back to warn his father's household not
to live for themselves and their own as he had done.
He was in torment, utterly alone. Meanwhile the
other picture shows the poor man Lazarus who once
lay at his gate. Without any family having cared for
him in this life, he was now with his father Abraham
and with the family of God in the next.

Let me just give you another little picture of
nepotism, this time in an African context. There is
much to excuse nepotism. Any man rising to a place
of importance in politics will be surrounded by relatives and friends looking confidently to him for pat-
ronage. The tradition of centuries leaves them in no
doubt that he will provide for them, and that if jobs
don't exist, they will be created. He may grasp the
constitutional issue himself, but it is difficult for him
to explain it to his kinsmen. Consequently, the life
of ministers and other people of importance is made
burdensome by nagging and increasing demands as
they find themselves enmeshed in the familiar net of
family obligations. I have been told in depressed
tones by ministers in both Nigeria and Ghana that
about half of a minister's life seems to consist of getting people jobs, even down to the grade of messen-
gers and office cleaners, a circumstance that might
well surprise ministers in Whitehall. Now why is
that?

One of the reasons has to do with the African view
of the afterlife. The African sees that there are three
kinds of existence: the living, the dead, and the

unborn. These are linked indissolubly with the land and with what happens in this life. They view the afterlife as being populated by the spirits of the departed who are looking after the family interests here on earth, goading people and holding them back depending on how well they are doing for the clan or the family. Not surprisingly, it is almost impossible in Africa to combat nepotism. It is not just a question of helping one's family; it is a part of one's whole view of reality. No one is himself unless he is contributing to the welfare of the cycle within his own clan: the living, the dead, and the not yet born.

Jesus' teaching about the family, however, recognises its duties and obligations but puts the family second to loyalty to himself and all that he stands for. Jesus sees the family of God made up—not just of one's relatives—but of those who do the will of God. He teaches the resurrection of all—those who have done good, of whatever family, and those who have done evil, of whatever family. The answer to this short-sighted, here-and-now attitude of nepotism is to follow Jesus' teaching that 'whoever does the will of my Father in heaven is my brother and sister and mother' (Matt. 12:50) and fully to act as though we are all moving towards resurrection.

Nepotism Involves Financial Manipulation

The second encounter of Caiaphas and his family with Jesus came with the cleansing of the temple. The bazaars of the sons of Annas were overthrown as Jesus overturned the tables of the money-changers and drove out those who sold pigeons and doves at exorbitant prices (Matt. 21:12, 13). How accurate he was when he described the bazaars of the sons of Annas as a 'den of robbers'. Have you ever noticed how the sons of Annas used money to buy their revenge? They bought Judas for 30 pieces of silver; they hired people to stage the arrest in the garden and incite the crowd before Pilate; they bribed false witnesses at the trial; they gave large bribes to the soldiers to tell their deception about the disciples stealing the body; and about Pilate they said to the soldiers, 'If this report gets to the governor, we will satisfy him and keep you out of trouble' (Matt. 28:14). Nepotism works on the principle that every man has his price, even relatives. This led to the Cross of Jesus Christ. 'It would be good if one man died for the people' (John 18:14).

Nepotism Breaks Laws

Nepotism plays fast and loose with laws, rules, policies, justice. The irregular trial of Jesus mocked and travestied justice, and the blame lies with Caiaphas. Capital cases should have been tried during the daytime and the verdict reached during the daytime, but the trial of Jesus took place at night. It was not lawful for the council to sit on the eve of the Sabbath or during a festival, but clearly they did so at that time. There could be no case to answer without the agreement of two witnesses, but we are specifically told that two witnesses could not agree. No man could be convicted on his own testimony, but Jesus was convicted on his own testimony. There could be no sentence in capital cases on the same day as the trial, but Jesus was sentenced before the morning. There was compulsory provision for defence counsel and the opportunity to defend, but that didn't happen. And there was no observance of the special form for trial of blasphemy. All this is what nepotism does. It makes its own rules, those that apply to me and mine. Again we see nepotism leading to the death of Jesus, the death of the innocent Jesus by driving a horse and chariot through the just and fair procedures that were already there to guide the process of justice. In like manner people are being crucified in the twentieth century where nepotism acts in precisely the same way and sets aside the rules, the laws, the policies, and the procedures and acts in the interests of ourselves and our own.

Nepotism Shows Insensitivity

Finally, nepotism is unfeeling and callous towards others. Nepotism's great concern about its own leaves little sympathy for those outside the circle. When Judas came back and threw the 30 pieces of silver down, what was the response? 'What is that to us? That's your responsibility' (Matt. 27:4). And when they came and saw Jesus and the cross they had put there, were they sorry for him? No, they mocked him and said, 'He saved others, but he can't save himself' (Matt. 27:42). No one matters outside one's own family. In a sense, family is an extension of self, and the extended family can be extended selfishness.

What difference, then, does the Cross of Jesus Christ make to those enmeshed in nepotism? The classic case in the New Testament of nepotism is James and John. In Mark 10 the mother and the two brothers came to Jesus and said, 'Let one of us sit at your right and the other at your left in your glory' (Mark 10:37). They were unfeeling. They were insensitive about how their request would affect the other ten, and the other disciples grew angry. The story comes right in the middle of the occasion when Jesus is trying to command their attention to say that the Son of Man must go up to Jerusalem and be crucified. All James and John can think about is the seat on the right hand and the seat on the left. This is the time when Jesus says, 'You know that those who are regarded as rulers of the Gentiles lord it over them, and their high officials exercise authority over them. Not so with you. Instead, whoever wants to become great among you must be your servant, and whoever wants to be first must be slave of all' (Mark 10:42–44).

Now have you ever noticed at the Cross the interesting sequel to that episode? In John's gospel—remember John was one of the two brothers who wanted the places on the right and the left—Jesus looks down from the Cross at his own mother and says, 'Here is your son.' And he looks down at John and says to him about Mary, 'Here is your mother.' And the gospel says, 'From that time on, this disciple took her into his home' (John 19:26, 27). John is the only one of the four Evangelists who tells us that story about the Cross. We don't get it in Matthew, Mark, or Luke. John is the one of the four Evangelists who uses most the concept of being born again as the children of God. John is the only one of the four Evangelists who mentions Annas and the family connections in telling us about the Cross. All this suggests that John is saying, 'I was like that, but the Cross made a difference. I began to discover where my real family was at the Cross.'

It is interesting that in the Crucifixion story in Mark's gospel, the mother of John and James, called Salome, is present at the Cross, but absent from the burial. I suspect that she may have gone with John her son and Mary his new mother to look after her back in the city. It's a lovely picture, isn't it? The woman who was pushing her two boys for the right and the left seat on the throne is—by the time she comes to the Cross—with her son and his new mother Mary, patterning a new family concept that could totally revolutionise the world. Caiaphas, then, tells us about one way of doing things in life in regard to our own; and the Cross of Jesus shows us a totally different one. Where do we stand before the Cross? With the family of Caiaphas, mocking Jesus because he was not one of their own, or with the family of God learning the new relationships governed by love? Who is your brother? Who is your mother? Who is your sister? Who is your father? Jesus would say, 'Whoever does the will of God.'

CHAPTER 4

THE CHIEF PRIESTS

The first trial scene in the drama of the Cross takes place before the whole Sanhedrin, where Jesus was brought immediately after his arrest. The stage stirs with scheming and intrigue. The chief priests, the elders, and the teachers of the law have assembled to look for evidence against Jesus. Some sit listening carefully to the proceedings; others huddle in groups of two and three; servants hurriedly exit, dispatched on errands, while others enter to deliver messages to Caiaphas, the high priest who presides over the inquiry. Witness after witness is ushered in to testify falsely against Jesus, but each contradicts the one before.

In the centre stands Jesus, silent, unmoving, unruffled. As it becomes clear that no two witnesses can agree, Caiaphas grows increasingly agitated and finally calls a halt to the farce. Standing in front of Jesus, he asks, 'Are you not going to answer? What is this testimony that these men are bringing against you?' (Mark 14:60). Silence. Impatiently he rephrases his question, 'Are you the Christ, the Son of the Blessed One?' (Mark 14:61). This time Jesus answers. 'I am.' Jesus claims to be the Messiah, the Son of God, and as if that were not enough, he goes on to associate himself with God sitting in judgement, with all the apocalyptic accompaniments,

'And you will see the Son of Man sitting at the right hand of the Mighty One and coming on the clouds of heaven' (Mark 14:62).

The Sanhedrin can easily recognise this reference to the book of Daniel; they realise that Jesus is saying that those who are judging him will see him on the seat of judgement with the Almighty at the last day. Caiaphas recognises his cue and, clearly playing to the galleries, tears his clothes in horror. '"Why do we need any more witnesses?" he asked. "You have heard the blasphemy. What do you think?"' (Mark 14:63). Blasphemy! Condemn him! Put him to death! The cries intensify as the stage erupts into confusion. Some are spitting on Jesus; someone else blindfolds him; others are striking and taunting him. Taking their cue from Caiaphas, the guards close in and begin to beat him.

What turned the Sanhedrin, the supreme court of all Jewry, into a scene of near riot and a travesty of justice? When the priests and the guards had finished beating Jesus, they bound him, and dragged him before Pilate, who called it as he saw it: envy (Mark 15:10). Not some violation of an obscure Jewish law, not insurrection against the Roman government, not even the official charge of blasphemy against God, but the envy of Caiaphas and the priests—brought into sharp relief against the background of the love of Jesus—sent Jesus to the Cross.

The Nature of Envy

The New Testament has two words for envy. The first has both a good and a bad meaning. In its good sense it means a jealous zeal or ardour for someone or some cause. Paul uses the word this way when he tells the Corinthians, 'I am jealous for you with a godly jealousy' (II Cor. 11:2), and it is even used to describe the zeal for righteousness that motivated Jesus to drive the money-changers and pigeon sellers out of the temple courts (John 2:17). In its bad sense it means an envious jealousy or rivalry as when Paul again says to the Corinthians, 'For since there is jealousy and quarrelling among you, are you not worldly?' (I Cor. 3:3). Zeal, even rivalry, is not a bad thing in itself, but it can easily be pushed too far or used for the wrong reasons. Then it becomes that possessive, clutching, mean thing called jealousy— love that begins to feed on itself. When zeal goes that far, it becomes something wholly bad.

The second New Testament word for envy is never used in a good sense. It means a vindictive, resentful rivalry, a covetous possessiveness. It is no longer concerned just to have what the other one has. It wants to prevent the other from having it as well. This is the word that Pilate used when he said that chief priests brought Jesus before him out of envy.

The Provocations of Envy

What provoked envy in the chief priests during the

last five days of Jesus' life? It all started when principle clashed with profit. At the beginning of that first Holy Week Jesus cleansed the temple, driving out the money-changers, overturning the benches of those selling pigeons and doves. It was a bold move against an established religious racket. It disrupted business and destroyed profits during the Passover festival. The sons of Annas stood to take a large loss in temple revenue. Why did Jesus do it?

He saw the temple as a house of prayer; the priests saw it as a lucrative business. He wanted all people of all nations to worship without restrictions; the priests restricted worship to the rich, to those who could afford to pay exorbitant fees for sacrificial animals. Jesus' stand on principle provoked the chief priests' envy, and they reacted in fear. His goodness threatened them. 'The chief priests and the teachers of the law heard this and began looking for a way to kill him' (Mark 11:18).

Envy is always aroused against the man who cannot be bribed, the one who will not compromise his principles. When Aristides the Just was on trial in Athens, a man came to ask another to register his vote for banishment. 'What harm has he done you?' asked the second, and the first replied, 'I am tired of hearing him called the Just.' Inevitably we envy the person who has the good qualities we should possess but don't. We hate to see that person and wish him out of our way.

Popularity also provokes envy. 'They feared him, because the whole crowd was amazed at his teaching' (Mark 11:18). 'The large crowd listened to him with delight' (Mark 12:37). Jesus clearly had the people on his side. All during that week he was drawing the big crowds, and the chief priests were reduced to spectators at the back. Popularity with a group or an important individual always incenses the envious person. When someone new gains the acceptance that he once had or cannot win, then envy takes over.

Performance provokes envy. Not only was Jesus drawing the crowds, but he was beating the teachers of the law at their own game. When the Pharisees asked Jesus whether or not it was lawful to pay taxes to Caesar, he answered so cleverly—'Give to Caesar what is Caesar's and to God what is God's'—that they were amazed at him (Mark 12:17). When the Sadducees asked their question about marriage in the resurrection, Jesus pointed out their ignorance of the law and started teaching them. 'Are you not in error because you do not know the Scriptures or the power of God? When the dead rise, they will neither marry nor be given in marriage; they will be like the angels in heaven. Now about the dead rising—have you not read in the book of Moses, in the account of the bush, how God said to him, "I am the God of Abraham, the God of Isaac, and the God of Jacob"? He is not the God of the dead, but of the living. You are badly mistaken!' (Mark 12:24–27).

When another teacher of the law asked him, 'Of all the commandments, which is the most important?' Jesus gave such a good answer—'Love the Lord your God with all your heart and with all your soul and with all your mind and with all your strength. The second is this: Love your neighbour as yourself. There is no commandment greater than these' (Mark 12:30, 31)—that 'from then on no one dared ask him any more questions' (Mark 12:34). It was a *tour de force* teaching performance, a demonstration of insight, wisdom, knowledge of the Scriptures, clear convictions, skilful debate, and gracious speech. In short, he was all that they as priests and leaders of the people should have been but were not. Jesus had even pointed out the discrepancy between their profession and their performance when he said, 'Watch out for the teachers of the law. They like to walk around in flowing robes and be greeted in the marketplaces, and have the most important seats in the synagogues and the places of honour at banquets. They devour widows' houses and for a show make lengthy prayers. Such men will be punished most severely' (Mark 12:38–40). Like an arrow at a target, envy shoots straight for the person who can do what we ought to be doing but are not.

The Methods of Envy

In the Chapel of the Arena at Padua stands a significant fresco of Envy by Giotto. It pictures a mean, misshapen man, with crouching shoulder and craning neck, lean, sunken cheeks, and sunken, averted eyes. One hand clutches a wallet of gold; the other stretches out with fingers shaped into claws. The ears are large, unshapely, distended. Out of the mouth winds a serpent whose fangs are striking Envy himself on the brow. Around the feet leap up flames of fire. This allegorical masterpiece depicts both the methods and the consequences of envy.

The large distended ears signify that envy is alert for every bit of slander or gossip. The serpent in the mouth points to the poisonous insinuations and fabricated stories which the tongue of envy eagerly tells. The hands clawed like a vulture's suggest the clutching greed and the violent, tearing motion of the envious spirit. The serpent striking Envy's own brow shows that envy really harms only itself, and the flames of fire round the feet mark the self-torture in which envy lives. In their treatment of Jesus the chief priests used all these methods and suffered the inevitable consequences of envy.

First the chief priests tried to trap Jesus in his talk. Pretending genuine interest, they asked insincere questions, hoping to trick him. They asked, 'By what authority are you doing these things?' (Mark 11:28). He had sprung the trap on them by refusing to answer until they told him from whom John had received his authority (Mark 11:31–33). When they asked him about paying taxes to Caesar, again he sprang the trap on them, 'and they were amazed at him' (Mark 12: 15–17). No matter how hard they tried, Jesus was too quick for them.

The clutching, tearing greed of envy's claw has no moral scruples. When the chief priests could not trap him in the daylight by their skill, they decided to try it at night by force. 'The Passover and the Feast of Unleavened Bread were only two days away, and the chief priests and the teachers of the law were looking for some sly way to arrest Jesus and kill him' (Mark 14:1). When Judas came to them to betray Jesus, 'they were delighted to hear this and promised to give him money' (Mark 14:11). Bribery, stealth, violence—envy scruples at nothing to achieve its end, nor does the grasping, tearing claw ever release its relentless clutching. 'Envy's a sharper spur than pay,' said John Gay; and 'Envy never makes holiday,' said Francis Bacon. Stricken by remorse, Judas could attempt restitution and return the money, but driven relentlessly on, the chief priests could not give up their envy.

When they had arrested him by force at night and brought him into the Sanhedrin, they did not hesitate to manipulate the rules of judicial procedure. An old manuscript called the Mishna, written about AD 200 by the patriarch Rabbi Juda, codifies the oral law and gives the rules of evidence and procedure in Jewish courts. Legal authorities generally agree that it reflects the customs that would have been in force during the time of Jesus.

A comparison of the rules of procedure in the Mishna with what actually happened to Jesus before the Sanhedrin reveals several striking irregularities. Before there could be a case to answer in a Jewish court, two witnesses had to come forward independently and agree in their evidence. On the basis of that agreement a case was then formulated and tried. The first witness was called to give evidence and to be interrogated. When he left, the next one was brought in. The court searched for agreement between two witnesses, but until such agreement was forthcoming, there was no case against Jesus. As the Sanhedrin tried Jesus, the chief priests brought in many witnesses, even false witnesses, seeking evidence on which to base a case against Jesus, 'but their statements did not agree' (Mark 14:56). Up to that point in the trial, according to Jewish law, there was no case to answer. Even so, Caiaphas began to question Jesus directly, 'Are you going to answer? What is this testimony that these men are bringing against you?' (Mark 14:60). Quite within his legal rights, Jesus answered nothing.

Again Caiaphas manipulated the rules by interrogating Jesus directly and convicting him on his own evidence. According to Jewish law no man could be convicted on his own testimony, yet when Jesus said that he was the Messiah, he was convicted of blasphemy based on his own testimony. Furthermore, Caiaphas ignored the special form of trial prescribed in the Mishna for cases of blasphemy, a particularly grievous offence in Jewish culture. Instead Caiaphas asked for an immediate verdict and found him guilty.

The distended ears of envy also thrive on gossip and slander and discord. When they brought Jesus to Pilate, 'the chief priests accused him of many things' (Mark 15:3). Those accusations ranged from hearsay and gossip to outright slander. When the crowd arrived to ask for the customary release of a prisoner at the festival, 'the chief priests stirred up the crowd to have Pilate release Barabbas' (Mark 15:11). The poison of envy, like the venom of the snake, infests everyone it strikes. There is no quarantine against envy.

Finally, envy revels in the defeat of its enemy, but in the end realises only self-defeat and inner torture. As Jesus hung on the Cross, 'the chief priests and the teachers of the law mocked him among themselves. "He saved others," they said, "but he can't save himself!"' Ironically, their mocking words simply condemned themselves and revealed the self-torture of envy. Jesus had saved others. He had saved Peter, Andrew, James, and John from a paltry life lived only for self; he had saved Levi from a shady, dishonest business; he had saved Peter's mother-in-law from a fever that incapacitated her; he had saved a leper from disease and social ostracism; he had saved the paralytic from guilt that had paralysed his limbs; he had saved the daughter of Jairus from an early death in girlhood, he had saved the epileptic boy, and his father, distraught by his terrible fits; he had saved Bartimeus from his blindness; he saved the repentent thief from a despairing death; he had come, in fact, 'to seek and to save what was lost' (Luke 19:10). He had saved others, but he had not saved the chief priests. Why?

Envy thinks only about itself. For the chief priests, 'self first' summed up their creed in life. When they said to Jesus, 'he can't save himself,' it was a jibe, a taunt, a sneer: the lowest, most despicable, most scornful thing they could think to say, judged by their own values. The sunken, averted, selfish eyes of envy could see no other values. It did not occur to them that man could live by any other creed. Jesus, however, had taught another principle of life which he followed to the end: 'For whoever wants to save his life will lose it, but whoever loses his life for me and for the gospel will save it' (Mark 8:35). He could not save himself precisely because he was saving others. He lost himself, but in the end gained for us eternal life. In contrast, the chief priests, their hearts burning with the covetousness of their selfish creed like the flames of torture licking around the feet of Envy, saved themselves—their temple rackets and their pride—but lost eternal life.

The Cure of Envy

Envy put Jesus on the Cross, but the cure for envy is found in the Cross. Jesus died not just to forgive our sins, but to free us from sin. Envy originates in the warped heart of man (Mark 7:22), the heart twisted inward in selfishness, but Jesus died to free us from the grasping clutch and venomous sting of envy. Hanging there on the Cross, he exposed himself to the envy of the chief priests. He suffered its full force and drew its sting. On the Cross he showed forever that 'love does not envy' (I Cor. 13:4), and he came back in the power of the Resurrection to transform our hearts from envy to love.

CHAPTER 5

PILATE: TRUTH AND POLITICS

That little phrase 'suffered under Pontius Pilate' has from the beginning been recited in the creeds of the Church and has possibly been translated into more languages around the world than even the Bible. Although that obscure Roman governor of Judaea stepped onto the stage of human history for only four hours, his name is known to more people in the world than those of most of the great men in history. What part did Pilate play in the drama of the Cross on that first Good Friday between eight o'clock and twelve noon? The answer lies in two statements recorded in Matthew's account: Pilate's own $64,000 political question, 'What shall I do, then, with Jesus who is called Christ?' (Matt. 27:22); and his wife's urgent message to him as he sat on the judgement seat, 'Don't have anything to do with that innocent man' (Matt. 27:19). Pilate tried to follow his wife's advice about Jesus, but he, like every man who has attempted it since, found this course of neutrality difficult.

The Paralysis of an Untidy Past

He suffered, in the first place, from his past. Pilate was not a high-born Roman. He was of the middle rank that we call the equestrian order. He had served in the army in Germany, and during a prolonged stay in Rome he seems to have captured the affection of a Roman girl of very high connections. She was Claudia Procula, the illegitimate daughter of Claudia, who was the third wife of the Emperor Tiberius and therefore the granddaughter of Augustus Caesar—we might say—on the wrong side of the blanket. This connection with the man at the top served Pilate's interests in an unexpected degree, for in AD 26, on the recommendation of Sejanus, Tiberius' right-hand man, he was appointed procurator of Judaea. Luke 3:1 tells us that Pilate was governor of Judaea when John the Baptist began his ministry, thus he would have been there for about four years when Jesus was brought to him. In taking up his post, he was allowed the very unusual privilege of taking his wife with him out to Judaea. So Pilate's appointment was what we call a nepotistic appointment. He had connections with the right family.

Procurator was not normally a top appointment, but in Judaea it carried more responsibility than in other places. He was responsible for law and order, for the administration of justice and for the collection of taxes. Like many men appointed in this nepotistic way of family favouritism, he was not quite up to the job. He was somewhat coarse, tactless, and a very obstinate man. To him, it seemed, authority meant the power to enforce his will, rather than the exercise of responsibility and consideration for others. He was the embodiment of that personal aggressiveness which men and women, thrust into positions of authority that exceed their powers, so often use to attain their ends. Let me illustrate.

In Jerusalem, when he arrived, it was the practice not to bring the usual Roman standards into Jerusalem because they had a picture of the Roman emperor on them. The Jews abhorred anything that signified graven images, and especially to bring these into the temple area would have been blasphemy to them because of the second commandment. Up until then it had been the Roman practice to respect this religious conviction and to use their standards without this picture in Jerusalem. But Pilate, when he came, was not for kowtowing to these superstitious Jews, and he sent the usual Roman standards into Jerusalem with a legion at night. When the people discovered the standards the next day, terrific crowds gathered ready to riot. They surrounded Pilate's house at Caesarea down at the coast; he in turn surrounded them with troops to try to get them to disperse. So sure were the Jews that they were making the protest for the right thing that they lay on the ground for five days and five nights until eventually Pilate had to give up and withdraw the standards.

Again, in Jerusalem the water supply was always a problem. Pilate constructed an aqueduct to bring water into the city, and he thought, 'Since I am doing this for the benefit of these people, we'll use some of their money.' Thus he took some of the temple tax to pay for the aqueduct, this item of development that

he thought was in their interest. Again the people re-
belled and rioted. This time he sent his own people
in plain clothes with clubs and daggers into the
crowd, and at a signal they turned on the people,
clubbed them, and stabbed them. Many others were
killed in the stampede.

Luke 13:1 mentions that some Galileans had their
blood mingled with their sacrifices at Pilate's insti-
gation. We don't have any details about that, but it is
consistent with the rest that we know about Pilate.
Another incident happened in Samaria a few years
after the death of Jesus. A sensationalist prophet in-
vited the Samaritans to come to Mount Gerizim in
their territory and said that he would show them the
sacred vessels, like the Ark of the Covenant, and
other vessels that he said Moses had hidden in the
mountain. Some people came, and some of them had
spears and sticks. Pilate assumed that there would be
trouble and sent troops immediately. Many were
killed then and later. The Samaritans reported this to
Vitellius, the Syrian legate, and Pilate was recalled
and banished. In sum, during the four years or more
that he was in Judaea, he was unpleasantly involved
with the people in every single district in his pro-
vince. Luke 23:12 tells us that he even managed to be
at enmity with Herod.

So Pilate was a man devoted to holding on to a job
that he never would have had but for his connections
with the right family, a job in which he bungled one
thing after another. His past was untidy in the ex-
treme, but he seems not to have recognised it or
attempted to improve or rectify it. He blundered on,
probably feeling that he had done no wrong and that

in each case others were to blame. He did not know it, and you may not know it either, but that self-justifying, blaming-others attitude brings to a person a moral paralysis that incapacitates him. How, then, is our past? A tidy past comes from ruthless self-criticism, a readiness to see and admit our mistakes to ourselves and to others, and a consequent building up of wisdom and experience and aptitude. There are still people who do the wrong thing with Jesus Christ because they are unwilling to face up to the realities of their origins and their past behaviour. Pilate needs to be for them a warning.

By contrast, we see Jesus there that day in front of Pilate as the complete opposite. 'He always had the nature of God, but he did not think that by force he should try to become equal with God. Instead of this, of his own free will he gave up all that he had, and took the nature of a servant. He became like man and appeared in human likeness. He was humble and walked the path of obedience all the way to death—his death on the cross' (Phil. 2:6–8, GNB). There you have the two men: Pilate with the rank to which he never should have risen and Jesus with the rank to which he should never have descended. That's the picture on Good Friday.

The Pressure of an Unwelcome Problem

As well as a past he would rather have forgotten, Pilate had a present problem. Two nights before the Passover feast, it appears that Caiaphas got in touch with Pilate about the contemplated arrest and trial of

Jesus. With Pilate's position as shaky as it was, it wasn't difficult for Caiaphas to get him to agree that next morning he would merely rubber-stamp and ratify what the Jewish court had decided during the night and sanction the death penalty. Only Pilate could pronounce the death penalty. Apparently, his wife knew something about this because she dreamed about Jesus that night. He was up at dawn to attend to the matter, but when she woke, her dream troubled her and she sent him this urgent message, 'Don't have anything to do with that innocent man' (Matt. 27:19). What was Pilate to do? If he didn't please the Jews, they would riot, report to Rome, and perhaps he would lose his job. If he didn't please his wife, she was the emperor's relative, and if she so reported, he could still be out of a job. That was Pilate's dilemma, the unexpected and unwelcome problem that built up the pressure under which he had to do his job on that black Friday. Note that both of the pressures were of his own making. He had antagonised the Jews. He had accepted the job on his wife's connection. Now the birds were coming home to roost, and his sin was finding him out because of the clash of these two conflicting choices. Life does this, and when it does, God is in fact offering us mercy or judgement in the language we best understand, the language of the priorities to which we have committed ourselves.

By contrast we see Jesus, single-minded, straightforward, teaching the truth without regard to man. He knew no sin. He did no sin. In him was no sin. His thought that day was not for himself at all but for others; for the women he passed going up the hill to Calvary, whom he told not to weep; for the soldiers who pierced his hands and feet with the hammer and the nails, about whom he said, 'Father, forgive them, for they do not know what they are doing' (Luke 23:34); for the thief to whom he said, 'Today you will be with me in paradise' (Luke 23:43); for his mother below the Cross when he said to John, 'Here is your mother,' and to Mary, 'Here is your son' (John 19:26, 27). And during the trial his concern, as we read the text, was for Pilate. See the contrast: Pilate thinking about his own interests— should he please his wife? should he please the Jews?—and in front of him Jesus who pleased not himself but in the end thought only of others.

The Pantomime of an Uncontrolled Plot

Pilate set out to follow his wife's advice, and he tried very hard. He wasn't going to be an automatic rubber stamp. When the Jews came, quite unexpectedly instead of his just saying, 'All right, I confirm the death penalty,' he said, 'What accusation do you bring?' They were surprised. They had expected the rubber stamp, and they said, 'Why? We wouldn't have brought him to you if he had not been guilty.' But he said, 'All right, take him and judge him by your own law.' And they came back, 'He teaches insurrection from Galilee.' At the word 'Galilee' Pilate said, 'Is he a Galilean? Send him to Herod.' He tried to have nothing to do with him by sending him to Herod. Herod dealt with him in the arrogant way that Herod had and sent him back with the message

'I don't find any fault in the man.' Pilate was still trying to do what his wife had urged and was ready to release him. He said, 'I normally give you someone to be released at this time. Why don't you have him?' And they said, 'No, give us Barabbas.' As a result he was again foiled, still trying to have nothing to do with Jesus.

Still vacillating, he decided, 'All right, I shall arrange a token punishment for him.' So he had him scourged and brought him out to the people looking abject in his suffering. Hoping to appeal to their sympathy, he said, 'Behold the man. Behold your king.' But they were not to be pressured. 'We have no king but Caesar, and if you let this man go, you are not Caesar's friend.' Eventually he delivered him up to be crucified, to be nailed to a cross by his hands and his feet, and hoisted to hang there, suspended between earth and heaven, until he died for all to gaze upon. That is what Pilate did.

That was the end of what I call 'Pilate's parade'. Read it in John's gospel; it does read like a tragic pantomime, complete with stage directions: 'Pilate came out to them' (John 18:29), 'Pilate then went back inside' (18:33), 'he went out again to the Jews' (18:38), 'once more Pilate came out' (19:4), 'he went back inside' (19:9), 'he brought Jesus out' (19:13). All this movement occurs in the narrative as John told it—and John was an eyewitness—but to what purpose? Why all this going in and going out when he ended up by delivering him to be crucified? He was trying to have nothing to do with Jesus as his wife advised. He tried hard, but he couldn't control events this time. Caiaphas was too clever; the people were too easily manipulated; Jesus was not co-operative. And the truth was that Jesus was not a threat to security, although they alleged it. Pilate was very impressed by his bearing. He was afraid of his dignity and his possible origin. He found no fault in him, and maintained that Jesus had done nothing worthy of his death. That was the truth. But the politics were different; he could have lost his job. And politics won.

Could it be that we know the truth? We see what is just and right and fair, but dare not say so or act rightly because something about us is threatened? We know the panic that Pilate felt and the events that he could not control, but he is also a lesson to us in what happens if we play the game that puts Jesus on the Cross and sends us into everlasting shame and loss like Pilate. By contrast we see Jesus, dishevelled but dignified. When he was reviled, he reviled not again; when he suffered, he did not threaten. He never said a word, made no unnecessary movement, remained calm yet bearing in his body our sins to the tree; naked with nothing but wounds to cover him, yet in perfect control.

The Pathos of an Unconscious Puppet

It was after this that Pilate took water and washed his hands before the crowd and said, 'I am innocent of this man's blood. It is your responsibility!' (Matt. 27:24). He still thought that he had done nothing with Jesus when he was the only man in the city who could pass the death sentence. That same self-

deceived atttitude persists through the narrative.
When they came and complained about what he had
written above the Cross, he said, 'What I have written, I have written' (John 19:22). When they came
and said, 'Will you take special care to seal the
tomb?' he replied, 'Go, make the tomb as secure as
you know how' (Matt. 27:65). When they asked for
anything, he returned the responsibility to them. He
was completely self-deceived, to the end unteach-
able. The centre of his deception was that he was not
responsible; it was others' fault; he was pushed into
the thing.

If we take that attitude to life, it is fatal. We need
to own our decisions. If we go that drifting way,
blaming others, saying they are responsible, the tremendous evil forces in the world will always push us
in the wrong direction. The tide is flowing in an evil
direction, and it always leads to some form of
Crucifixion of Jesus. That's why Jesus said, 'He who
is not with me by choice is against me by non-
choice.'

I remember as a young man going to a Youth for
Christ rally in Glasgow, and the preacher an-
nounced his text for the next night. He was going to
preach on 'What must I do to be lost?' As a young,
budding preacher, I thought, 'That's a good sermon
title. I'm going to hear it.' The next night he got up
and said, 'What must I do to be lost? Nothing.' His
text? 'How shall we escape, if we neglect so great a
salvation?' To neglect is to do nothing. Pilate tried to
do nothing, and his refusal to choose led to the
Cross, recall to Rome, and banishment to Vienne on
the Rhône in France, where he died a suicide's death.

Peace and Pardon

By contrast we see Jesus in total control. 'No man takes my life from me. I lay it down of myself.' And he did. He was the willing sacrifice, having been tempted in all points as we are, yet without sin that he might present himself without spot to God; having suffered that he might become the perfect offering for imperfect you and me and Pilate, owning what he did, setting his face as a flint to go to Jerusalem, choosing death, not drifting into it, choosing death because it was what needed to be done that you and I might be saved from our sins and given eternal life with God.

This message of salvation, of peace, of unconditional pardon, formed the theme of the disciples' early preaching. When, 50 days later, these disciples went out into the streets, Peter made the point unequivocally to the people: 'You handed him over to be killed, and you disowned him before Pilate' (Acts 3:13). 'You acted in ignorance, as did your leaders' (Acts 3:17). But he went on to say, 'Repent, then, and turn to God, so that your sins may be wiped out' (Acts 3:19). In other words, he was saying, although you were like Pilate and Pilate was like you, and although you are equally responsible, admit it and you can be forgiven. The guilt doesn't need to go on as it did with Pilate until it leads to a suicide.

The message of the day of Pentecost was that even if we are involved in Jesus' death, we can still be unconditionally forgiven if we admit our guilt and come to him. Life doesn't need to end as it did for Pilate. We need to let all family and political and other considerations go, and come boldly to Christ for whatever we have done wrong, for there is forgiveness in him. If Good Friday means anything, it ought to mean a renewal, a renewed sense or a new sense that, as the song says, 'My sin—O the bliss of the glorious tho't! My sin—not in part, but the whole, Is nailed to his cross and I bear it no more; Praise the Lord, Praise the Lord, O my soul!' Let us kneel in spirit at the foot of the Cross until we feel the cord snap that binds the burden of guilt to our weary backs. Let us feel the release as it rolls away. Let us savour the wonder of being forgiven again, the ecstasy of being set free, and then let us stand and walk and run and dance in our new-found joy as we sing with the pilgrim in Bunyan's story, 'Blessed cross, blessed sepulchre, but blessed rather be the man who there was crucified for me.'

CHAPTER 6

THE CROWD AND BARABBAS

The shouts of 'Hosanna in the highest!' faded into silence as the echo came reverberating back through the darkness of the Good Friday dawn, 'Crucify him! Crucify him!' In the flickering firelight of the soldiers' torches, the scourge and crown of thorns threw distorted shadows like palm branches against the walls of Pilate's palace, while the cries of 'Blessed is the King of Israel!' became jumbled and twisted into the mocking refrain, 'We have no king but Caesar.' From applause and adulation to scorn and spitting, the fickle crowd wavered between Palm Sunday and Good Friday as Pilate offered them a choice between Jesus and Barabbas. What swayed the crowd who wanted Pilate to release Barabbas to freedom and to sentence Jesus to death?

The narrative in Mark 15 suggests an established practice of trying to placate the people—'Now it was the custom at the Feast to release a prisoner whom the people requested' (v 6)—followed by a plain fact: 'A man called Barabbas was in prison with the insurrectionists who had committed murder in the uprising' (v 7). The crowd came to ask for the customary release (v 8). This may have been the real purpose for the crowd's coming together, not primarily for the trial of Jesus but rather for the release of a prisoner. Pilate offered Jesus to the crowd, thinking that Jesus was popular with the people and that only the priests desired his death (vv 9, 10). The priests engineered the demand for Barabbas (v 11). Pilate then attempted to prompt a demand for Jesus or, perhaps, even to offer them both Jesus and Barabbas (v 12). The unexpected answer came back, 'Crucify him!' (v 13). Convinced of his innocence, Pilate asked incredulously, '"Why? What crime has he committed?" But they shouted all the louder, "Crucify him!"' (v 14). The established practice of pleasing the crowd, regardless of principle, then asserted itself: 'Wanting to satisfy the crowd, Pilate released Barabbas to them. He had Jesus flogged, and handed him over to be crucified' (v 15).

What moved the crowd to choose Barabbas and to reject Jesus? Their choice can best be analysed by focussing on Barabbas, this man who did no deed and spoke no word in the gospel story, but whom the people chose instead of Jesus. Insignificant in himself, he casts a significant light on the people of that historic morning.

The Crowd's Choices

The crowd, first of all, made a casual choice. They had not come to ask for a specific person. They had no name in mind. They held no anger against Jesus of any long standing, for only days before they had waved their palm branches and shouted 'Hosanna!' as he rode into Jerusalem. The release was just one of the events of the festival. The choice was just group dynamics working in a crowd infected with holiday spirit. Pilate suggested Jesus; the priests pressed for Barabbas. Barabbas appealed to them, and they exercised their privilege of choosing the man to be released. It was a casual choice, lightly taken, not predetermined, but made on the spur of the moment.

The fact that their choice was casual, however, does not make it less significant. Psychologists tell us that the casual, unguarded, unpremeditated action gives the best clue to the real state of a person. The same principle applies to the crowd. Their snap decision offers a significant clue to the real situation, the underlying emotional reason for their choice of Barabbas.

An Emotional Choice

Consider the scene. Pilate, flanked by Roman soldiers and the Roman standard, stood on the steps of his palace, supreme symbol in Judaea of the hated occupying power of Rome. Before him stood Jesus, hands tied, eyes blindfolded, body bruised and beaten. More than a touch of irony must have crept into Pilate's voice as he asked the crowd, 'Do you want me to release to you the king of the Jews?' That same crowd had tried before in better circumstances to make Jesus king. After the feeding of the five thousand, says John, the crowd 'intended to come and make him king by force' (John 6:15). At the triumphal entry they had shouted, 'Blessed is the

King of Israel!' (John 12:13). That same crowd had no doubt cheered him on as he purged the temple and drove out the detested sons of Annas. Benches and tables overturned, pigeons flapping wildly in their cages, the money-lenders shouting and clutching their bags, children scrambling underfoot as coins spilled and rolled across the pavement—the crowd had enjoyed the spectacle then, the sense of power unleashed against an oppressive hierarchy. Now, however, Jesus stood there silent, not defending himself, a pitiful spectacle and symbol of their own subjugation.

Barabbas, on the other hand, was a rebel, a nationalist. He had taken part in an insurrection. He had struck a blow at Rome. He symbolised the freedom they longed for. His rebellion represented the political aspirations of the people to triumph over their colonial masters. Barabbas had committed murder. He believed in violence in the pursuit of his political goal, and for the crowd, as for many men since, that belief is attractive. See where non-violence had led Jesus, when earlier they could have made him king by force. Here was an opportunity to hit back at Pilate who wanted to foist on them the weak and unattractive Jesus whom even he had mocked with the title 'king of the Jews'. Yes, Barabbas suited their mood. He provided an emotional outlet for the frustrations of a subject people. He matched their deep-seated desire for freedom, and the crowd rose to the suggestion that he be released.

An Irrational Choice

The desire for freedom is not wrong. It is a basic drive of the human spirit, an emotional rallying point down through the centuries, and as such is good and right. Yet people ought to act not only instinctively, emotionally, but also rationally. In their choice of Barabbas, however, the crowd responded emotionally and irrationally. The priests had framed Jesus on a political charge in order to have him done away. They presented him to Pilate as the 'king of the Jews', an alleged threat to Roman rule. The crowd caught up the idea, shouting at Pilate, 'If you let this man go, you are no friend of Caesar. Anyone who claims to be a king opposes Caesar' (John 19:12). And again they cried, 'We have no king but Caesar' (John 19:15). On the one hand they professed allegiance to Caesar and seemed to support the Roman occupation. On the other hand they shouted for the release of Barabbas, an actual proven threat to Roman rule. The crowd did not detect the inconsistency of their own argument and were moved into this irrational, unthinking choice—showing little consideration at all of the issues.

An Irresponsible Choice

It follows logically that the crowd also made an irresponsible choice. It was a couldn't-care-less choice formed in the absence of any values to influence their decision. They did not appreciate the fact that they were sacrificing the best for something good, the right for the attractive, the spiritual for the material, or the eternal for the temporal. They had no values like that worked out. They were just a crowd. *Panis et circenses* was the sum of their existence: bread and circuses, food and entertainment, and work only as a means to either. They were a normal crowd, in a normal holiday spirit, and the outcome was not an unexpected event.

A Fatal Choice

Certainly the crowd did not realise in this brief encounter with Pilate that they had also made a fatal choice—fatal for justice, for right, truth, honour, integrity and nobility; fatal for Jesus; fatal for themselves. Their normal behaviour tended to fix truth forever on the scaffold and wrong forever on the throne. Oppression, injustice, prejudice, inequality, exploitation—all flourish in a casual, unthinking attitude towards life. Pilate tried to force the crowd to think about the issue of right and wrong when he asked, 'Why? What crime has he committed?' but the people only shouted all the louder, 'Crucify him!' (Mark 15:14). In the same way in the twentieth century we crucify justice and truth and nail oppressed and exploited peoples to the scaffold when our thoughtless attitude towards life blinds us to the issues of our time.

The crowd's normal behaviour was also fatal for Jesus. As a direct result of their choice Jesus died, the just Saviour for the unjust Barabbas. That is what we need to see: irrational and irresponsible behaviour is the very stuff out of which the Cross of Jesus was hewn. If you want to see the nature and end of this sort of behaviour, then come to Calvary. The nails that put Jesus there were forged of no different material. Think for a moment about this poem by G A Studdert Kennedy.

When Jesus came to Golgotha
   they hanged him on a tree,
They drove great nails through hands and feet,
   and made a Calvary;
They crowned him with a crown of thorns,
   red were his wounds and deep
For those were crude and cruel days
   and human flesh was cheap.

When Jesus came to Birmingham
   they simply passed him by,
They never hurt a hair of him,
   they only let him die;
For men had grown more tender,
   and they would not give him pain,
They only just passed down the street
   and left him in the rain.

Still Jesus cried, 'Forgive them,
   they know not what they do!'
And still it rained the wintery rain
   that drenched him through and through;
The crowds went home and left the streets
   without a soul to see,
And Jesus crouched against the wall
   and cried for Calvary.

The Cross does not placard the dastardly nature of heinous sins; rather it illumines, like the lightning flash that lights up the countryside, the true nature of all sin, or, if you like, the deadly nature of much normal behaviour. The attitude towards life of these people led them to choose Barabbas and to say of Christ, 'Crucify him!'

We easily disparage and sit in judgement over that Jewish crowd, but this kind of attitude towards life is also true of some of us. Emotional and careless—normal—like the ordinary run of people. Imagine a British crowd on a Bank Holiday Monday. If Christ were to return now, a British crowd would give him the same treatment as did that Jewish crowd on the first Good Friday. 'I wouldn't,' we protest—but we must prove it by doing the right thing with Jesus Christ now. 'Oh, that's different,' we say, 'that's not fair, that's putting me in a corner.' Yes, it is, but that is where some of us need to be put to face up to our unthinking attitude towards life and our casual treatment of Jesus Christ.

At the end of *Saint Joan* George Bernard Shaw makes this same analysis of normal human behaviour. In an epilogue to the play, set 25 years after the death of Joan, all those responsible for her execution, including a twentieth-century gentleman bringing news of her canonisation, come back to King Charles in a dream. One by one they kneel before Joan in a litany of praise: 'The girls in the field praise thee ... The dying soldiers praise thee ... The princes of the Church praise thee ... The judges in the blindness and bondage of the law praise thee ... The tormentors and executioners praise thee.' Joan interrupts their pious adoration, exclaiming, 'Woe unto me when all men praise me! I bid you remember that I am a saint, and that saints can work miracles. And now tell me: shall I rise from the dead, and come back to you a living woman?' One by one they make their excuses and apologies and leave the stage. Even the twentieth-century gentleman bows formally and withdraws, saying, 'The possibility of your resurrection was not contemplated in the recent proceedings for your canonisation. I must return to Rome for fresh instructions.' At the end of the play, Joan, bathed in a white radiance like Christ in his white robe before the judgement seat of Pilate, stands alone to deliver the closing lines. 'O God that madest this beautiful earth, when will it be ready to receive Thy saints? How long, O Lord, how long?' Few of us want to confront a saint, just as few of us want to confront Christ, for both shake us out of our comfortable, normal human behaviour and require us to do the right thing with Jesus Christ.

The crowd's choice was fatal for justice, fatal for Jesus, and fatal also for themselves. 'Let his blood be on us and on our children!' cried the crowd (Matt. 27:25), and in adopting Barabbas and his kind they set the wheels moving for their own destruction. This multitude did not know whom they were rejecting, and did not know that they were closing the book of their history, risking their eternal destiny and quenching with their own breath their one hope of temporal peace and spiritual greatness when they cried, 'Not this man but Barabbas.' Jerusalem defied Rome with a Barabbas attitude, and Rome destroyed Jerusalem and scattered the people into centuries, millennia of persecution and anti-Semitism. His blood was on them and their children.

The person who rejects Jesus Christ in a casual way comes under the judgement of God. When we will neither bow down before Christ's Cross nor bear it, we are in silence choosing our doom as decisively as though we had uttered the words, 'His blood be on us and on our children.' It is the cry of the condemned.

To the crowd Pilate said, 'What shall I do, then, with Jesus who is called Christ?' and the crowd answered, 'Crucify him!' To the crowd 50 days later Peter said, 'God has made this Jesus, whom you crucified, both Lord and Christ' (Acts 2:36); and their hearts were smitten with the realisation of what they had done and they cried, 'Brothers, what shall we do?' (Acts 2:37). To the crowd and to every man since who is willing to confront his careless attitude towards life—his normal behaviour that crucifies Christ and his saints—Peter answered, 'Repent and be baptised, every one of you, in the name of Jesus Christ so that your sins may be forgiven. And you will receive the gift of the Holy Spirit. The promise is for you and your children and for all who are far off—for all whom the Lord our God will call' (Acts 2:38, 39).

CHAPTER 7

THE ADULTERY OF HEROD

The third trial scene takes place in Herod's court. Surrounded by the chief priests and teachers of the law vehemently accusing him, Herod curiously questioning him, and the soldiers cruelly mocking him, Jesus dominates this scene by saying nothing. For Caiaphas he had had answers and prophecies, for Annas questions of legal rights, for Pilate truth and reasoning, for Peter a warning look—but for Herod silence. Herod is the only man to whom Jesus had nothing to say. What had Herod done to deserve the silent treatment? Both the Bible and secular history agree that the root of his trouble was his adultery; thus an answer to the question must begin here.

Herod's Career

Scripture mentions three Herods: Herod the Great, who was made king of the Jews by the Roman Senate in 40 BC and who appears in the nativity stories of the Magi and the slaughter of the innocents; Herod Antipas, who succeeded his father in 4 BC and who appears in the gospel stories; and in the Acts there was Herod Agrippa, who imprisoned Peter, executed James the brother of John, persecuted the Church, and was almost persuaded by Paul to become a Christian. In between was the second Herod, Herod Antipas, who is our man. We know little about his early life, but we can assume for a son of Herod the Great at least a formal training in the Jewish religion. At one point his father named him as sole heir to the whole kingdom, but later he divided the kingdom into four parts, giving Judaea to his son Archelaus, Iturea and Trachonitis to his stepson Philip, Abilene to Lysanias, and Galilee and Trans-Jordan to Herod Antipas—this division accounting for their title 'tetrarch', or ruler of one-fourth of the country.

Herod Antipas was a reasonable ruler from all accounts, not outstanding, but better than Archelaus his brother. Educated in Rome, he was a man of some culture and taste and had inherited his father's flair for building. The city of Tiberias, built by Herod and named after the emperor, still stands today. He married the daughter of Aretas, Arabian king of the nearby kingdom of the Nabataeans. About his marriage we know nothing except that it was formally and fully contracted.

Herod's Choice

It was after his training and marriage that the issue of his life arose. On a visit to his half-brother Philip in Rome, he fell in love with Philip's wife Herodias. After some talk about marriage, they negotiated an agreement: she would come to live with him if he would divorce his wife, the daughter of Aretas. Now Herod had to choose.

Would he obey the law of God? Mosaic law did allow a man to divorce his wife and a divorced woman to remarry (Deut. 24:1–4); thus Herod could have divorced his own wife and, if Philip had agreed to divorce Herodias (which is doubtful), Herodias could have remarried. Jesus, however, had removed this double standard in the Mosaic law. 'Anyone who divorces his wife and marries another woman commits adultery against her. And if she divorces her husband and marries another man, she commits adultery' (Mark 10:11, 12). Custom may dictate and society may behave as if there were a double standard, but Jesus declared that there is no double standard in God's eyes. Furthermore, whether or not Philip co-operated with Herod and Herodias, the Mosaic law still forbade their marriage—'If a man marries his brother's wife, it is an act of impurity; he has dishonoured his brother' (Lev. 20:21). Even if the brother were dead, Mosaic law would not have allowed Herod to marry Herodias because she had a child, the girl Salome.

Aside from the Mosaic prohibitions against marrying his brother's wife, Herod had to choose what to do with his own wife. Would he be faithful to his vows to the daughter of Aretas? Would he honour his word? And then there were the people. What sort of an example in this matter would he be to the people whom he ruled? Or would he ignore the implications for his subjects, renounce his vows to Aretas' daughter, reject the law of God, and take Herodias for his wife?

Herod was no fool. A responsible person who had shown good judgement in other matters, he knew the risks. It was unwise, even indecent, to marry such a close relative. His father had been estranged from his own wife, had ordered her to be executed, and then in sorrow and contrition had called her name through the corridors of the palace for weeks afterward. He was allying himself with a strong, scheming woman—witness the divorce clause in the marriage contract referred to above. What was he to do? He could stick by his first choice, honour God, be faithful to his wife, be a worthy father and ruler of a country; or he could follow his passions, defy God, wound his wife, make himself unfit as an example to those whom he governed, and take Herodias. He chose the second quite deliberately and quite calculatingly.

Herod's Chance

If anything is clear in the Gospel of Jesus Christ, it is that a single sin—even adultery—never damns a man. There is mercy with God. To the woman taken in adultery and brought to Jesus for condemnation, he said, 'Neither do I condemn you. Go now and leave your life of sin' (John 8:11). To the Samaritan woman who tried to fill the vacuum in her life with sex, Jesus offered the living water of forgiveness (John 4). In his parable of the prodigal son, the father reinstated the son unconditionally on his return in spite of the protests of the righteous brother (Luke 15:20–31). And to the self-righteous Pharisee who thanked God that he was not an adulterer, Jesus said that adulterers who knew and admitted their sin were more likely to enter the kingdom than those self-righteous Pharisees who refused to confront their sin (Luke 18:9–14). God does offer mercy, and Herod found that mercy in a man of God called John the Baptist.

John's fearless ministry had already brought forgiveness and repentance to thousands who came to be baptised. To the ordinary people he had said, 'The man with two tunics should share with him who has none, and the one who has food should do the same' (Luke 3:11). To the tax collectors he said, 'Don't collect any more than you are required to' (Luke 3:13). To the soldiers he said, 'Don't extort money and don't accuse people falsely—be content with your pay' (Luke 3:14). And to Herod he had said, 'It is not lawful for you to have your brother's wife' (Mark 6:18). That took courage. Jesus said, 'I tell you the truth: among those born of women there has not risen anyone greater than John the Baptist' (Matt. 11:11). Herod knew it was true and locked up John in prison. Herodias knew it was true and began to scheme for John's death.

Although Herod had shut up John in prison, he could not shut up his conscience. Here, then, was Herod's hope. 'Herod feared John and protected him, knowing him to be a righteous and holy man. When Herod heard John, he was greatly puzzled; yet he liked to listen to him' (Mark 6:20). A greater contrast than that between Herod and John could hardly be imagined. Herod was sensual; John was ascetic and disciplined, wearing animal skins and feeding on locusts and wild honey. Herod was ambitious; John had renounced worldly honour, giving place to Jesus, saying, 'One more powerful than I will come, the thongs of whose sandals I am not worthy to untie' (Luke 3:16). Herod was crafty and sly, earning from Jesus the epithet 'that fox' (Luke 13:32); John was blunt and direct. Herod epitomised worldliness; John epitomised courageous rectitude. Yet an irresistible attraction drew Herod to John. The religious and moral truth that John proclaimed repelled and puzzled and attracted him. He turned away, yet turned back. He locked him up in prison, yet brought him out to listen to him. Clearly at this point there was some hope for Herod, but every day that he gave in to Herodias and kept John in prison he drove another nail in his spiritual coffin.

It has been like that with many men and the teachings of Jesus ever since. We have dismissed as impractical Jesus' teachings on racial prejudice, economic exploitation, and war; yet we have not been able to put them away. We tell ourselves, surely God did not intend integration of our schools, or an equitable distribution of our wealth in the Third World, or an end to our nuclear armament? Yet, like persistent knocking that will not go away, the truth of God's Word attracts and puzzles and intrigues us. Like Herod, we lock up God's truth, yet are drawn irresistibly to listen and to choose.

Herod's Change

Herod had a chance, but he waited too long. 'Herodias nursed a grudge against John and wanted to kill him' (Mark 6:19). Herodias, too, had been waiting, and now the opportune time had arrived—a birthday banquet with Herod's high officials and military commanders and the leading men of Galilee present. She was astute in her choice of the situation. She would ask Herod for John's death in front of all the important people in his kingdom. She was astute in her method—a seductive dance—for Herod was clearly vulnerable there as she well knew. She was astute in her timing. Pleased with the dance, Herod had rashly promised Salome, 'Ask me for anything you want, and I'll give it to you.' Then swearing an oath, he had added, 'Whatever you ask I will give you, up to half my kingdom' (Mark 6:22, 23). When the girl turned to her mother, Herodias was ready with an answer, 'The head of John the Baptist on a platter' (Mark 6:25).

What was Herod to do? He had sworn an oath, and he did not want to break his word. He had made a promise in front of many important people, and he did not want to lose face. His pride and prestige were at stake. Like many people after him, for whom a brave show before the crowd has been more important than moral distinctions, Herod sent an executioner with orders to bring back John's head. How noble a terrible act can be made to look. Keeping his word had suddenly become extremely important, yet it was too late. Herodias, the living symbol of his broken word, had successfully schemed a second time to make him break a moral law. Against his better judgement he surrendered to the stratagems of the woman whom he had chosen to replace his first wife. This was Herod's crisis, and he failed. The execution of John the Baptist silenced the voice of God.

Herod's Condemnation

When Jesus stood silently before Herod very early in the morning of the Crucifixion, the past suddenly became present. Just as Herod had listened curiously to John the Baptist, so 'for a long time he had been wanting to see Jesus' (Luke 23:8). Some people were saying that Jesus was John raised from the dead (Luke 9:7–9), and Herod was perplexed. Perhaps, prodded by some last shred of conscience, he even secretly hoped that it were true. More likely he simply wanted to be entertained by some spectacle, to see Jesus perform a miracle (Luke 23:8). 'He plied him with many questions, but Jesus gave him no answer' (Luke 23:9).

What did Herod ask Jesus? Would it be stretching a point too far to suppose that Herod asked about John the Baptist? Was John really a prophet? Had John been right and Herod wrong about Herodias? Should he have listened to John after all? We don't know what Herod did ask Jesus, but we do know that others who have delayed too long the choice between right and wrong have wished that they could have a second chance, have wished that they could make a crucial decision over again and in hindsight have long agonised over what they should have done.

As Herod questioned the silent Jesus, his own conscience accused him and found him guilty. But Jesus said nothing. For the thief on the cross, he had salvation; for the soldiers he had forgiveness; for the women he had care; for John and his mother he had concern; yet for Herod he had nothing. Not even a word. Herod had silenced the voice of God. With roles reversed, Jesus no longer stood before Herod the judge, but Herod stood before Jesus the judge. And Herod acted with the only weapons left to him—mockery and ridicule and contempt—the defence mechanism of the seared conscience. Once again Herod faced a moral crisis and failed, and he sent Jesus back to Pilate.

Herod's End

Herod's demise after this event is significant. The divorce of his first wife had provoked a war with Aretas that destroyed Herod's army. According to Josephus the people regarded this defeat as divine judgement upon Herod for the murder of John. When Herod went to Rome to plead for the kingship of the Jews, he was charged with misrule and was exiled to Gaul where he died in AD 39. Herod Agrippa came into Caesar's favour, and Herodias was green with envy. Josephus writes of her that 'she was grieved and much displeased ... she was not able to conceal how miserable she was ... she could not bear to live any longer while Agrippa prospered and her husband did not. Thus did God punish Herodias for envy at her brother and Herod also for giving ear to the vain discourses of a woman.' Thus Herod died, incapacitated from making right judgements by foolish weakness, by stubborn pride, and by moral bankruptcy. He had silenced the voice of God.

CHAPTER 8

PETER'S DENIAL

While Jesus stood centre stage to face first Caiaphas, then Pilate, then Herod, Peter waited in the wings, watching. A player, but not yet involved in the play, Peter stood trying to decide what part to play. Christians identify more closely with Peter than with any other character in the whole New Testament, and curiously we tend to identify with him not in his strengths, but in his idiosyncrasies and weaknesses. Perhaps that is why he is there in the drama of the Cross. We identify with him especially in the trial scene and in his denial of Jesus. We know that it could have been us. Maybe we know that it has been us. The issue was whether he would identify with Jesus in alien, hostile company. To deny meant just to refuse to be identified with Jesus.

> While Peter was below in the courtyard, one of the servant girls of the high priest came by. When she saw Peter warming himself, she looked closely at him.
>
> 'You also were with that Nazarene, Jesus,' she said.
>
> But he denied it. 'I don't know or understand what you're talking about,' he said, and went out into the entryway.
>
> When the servant girl saw him there,

she said again to those standing around, 'This fellow is one of them.' Again he denied it.

After a little while, those standing near said to Peter, 'Surely you are one of them, for you are a Galilean.'

He began to call down curses on himself, and he swore to them, 'I don't know this man you're talking about.' (Mark 14:66–71)

Yes, change the time and the place, and it could have been us. We do identify with Peter in his denial. We are glad that he was there in the events leading up to Calvary, for if he was there, perhaps there is a place there for us also.

Now this denial is a clear issue, and we must look at it for our own good. How did it arise? It arose first of all out of conflicting estimates of Peter. The story begins with an assessment by Jesus of the disciples, and of Peter in particular, in Mark 14:27.

'You will all fall away,' Jesus told them, 'for it is written:
 "I will strike the shepherd,
   and the sheep will be scattered."
But after I have risen, I will go ahead of you into Galilee.'

Peter declared, 'Even if all fall away, I will not.'

'I tell you the truth,' Jesus answered, 'today—yes, tonight—before the rooster

crows twice you yourself will disown me
three times.'

But Peter insisted emphatically, 'Even
if I have to die with you, I will never disown you.' (Mark 14:27–31)

So we have two estimates of Peter: Jesus' estimate—
the true one as the events show—and his own self-
confident estimate—the false one as the events
show.

This was not the first time. Peter had experienced
problems with self-confidence before. Just go back.
Do you remember the incident on the lake recorded
in Luke 5 when Jesus found the disciples having
toiled all night and having caught nothing? He told
them to go out and cast the net on the right side of
the boat. Peter's response was 'That's stupid. We
know about fishing. You don't. But again, nevertheless, at your will we will go out.' To his surprise
Jesus was right. Or remember the matter of the temple tax. 'Should we pay the temple tax?' 'Yes, of
course,' said Peter to the inquirers, but Jesus had to
say to him, 'Not so fast, Peter.' And eventually it
was sorted out.

The Lure of the Bait

Even after he had made his famous confession of
Christ, Peter's self-confidence got him in trouble.
Jesus had told them and Peter in particular that he
was going up to the Cross. Peter's response was,

'No, no, that's not for you, Lord.' Jesus had to say to him, 'Wait a minute, Peter. What I'm saying is right. What you are saying is wrong.' In fact, it was, as we look back, becoming a pattern—Jesus right, Peter wrong. It was almost as though Peter was counting too early on the fulfilment of Jesus' prophecy that he would be Peter instead of Simon. He had heard that prophecy at the beginning. 'And I tell you that you are Peter, and on this rock I will build my church, and the gates of Hades will not overcome it' (Matt. 16:18). Perhaps this had gone to his head. This night he is still confident in himself, still believing in himself, believing himself to be what only existed in his imagination. Don't we all do that? We believe ourselves to be the person we think we are. That's wishful thinking—not always bad, but sometimes dangerous. This self-confidence based on a false estimate of himself, then, lured Peter into trouble the night before Calvary. 'I won't deny you. I'll show you.'

It proved to be quite a night. As time went on he fell asleep. He was warned: 'Peter, are you not able to stay awake one hour?' And we hear echoes of 'How is the denying going to work out when you can't even stay awake?' Then, true to character, when they got into the Garden and the soldiers came to arrest Jesus, Peter drew out his sword to defend Jesus and cut off the ear of the high priest's servant. 'I'll show them.' He was still in that self-confident mode and, of course, was rather put off when Jesus intervened and said, 'No, swords are not for now.' And then when they all forsook him and fled, Peter stayed the course and followed on. His presence there was his assertion that his own estimate of himself was true.

Should he have been there? Had he been asked to follow? In general, Jesus had said to them, 'When they persecute you in one city, flee to the next.' In particular, Jesus had said to them that night, 'You will be scattered.' But Peter wasn't for being part of the scattering. He followed on. It is interesting to think it through. Should he have been there at all? Should he have been there but have remained unobtrusive and unnoticed like John? Should he have been there and advertised outright that he belonged to Jesus? Or should he have been there and admitted his connection only when asked? You can take your pick. It is difficult to answer that, but not unimportant, not only in arriving at a verdict about Peter, but also in arriving at a verdict about ourselves.

Anyway it is clear what brought him there: an inadequate knowledge about himself; a persistent, but unwarranted opinion about himself. Where did he go wrong? Clearly, he was not profiting from the past as much as he might; he was not reading his mistakes and correcting them. As a result he still believed himself to be the person in his imagination and was not looking closely enough at the hard evidence of his life. Peter confused what he was when he was alone with what he was when he was in company. Peter confused what he was with congenial company with what he was in alien or other company. He confused what he was when he was with equals, like the other disciples, with what he would be when he was with others who were, socially at least, his superiors. Maybe he also confused what he was with his inferiors with what he was with his superiors, for we can be two different people depending on whether we are relating up or relating down. Most significantly, he confused what he was in talk with what he was in fact, and the bait of his own good opinion of himself lured and enticed him into the trap until he was caught.

He was not the first, nor will he be the last. It seems almost characteristic in the Bible. Joseph had grandiose dreams about himself before he emerged from his long imprisonment the man that God wanted him to be. Moses was going to rectify singlehandedly the wrongs of his countrymen, but his grandiose plan led him 40 years to the backside of the desert before he was ready. It is almost a pattern, a stage we have to go through, to lose our confidence in ourselves so that it may be placed elsewhere in God. So it was with Peter. Conflicting estimates, then, set the scene: what Jesus said Peter was going to do and what Peter professed he was able to do.

The Springing of the Trap

How did it happen? He had started out well that night, determined to follow Jesus, trying hard to be true to what he said he was going to be, standing there by the fire with his teeth clenched and all his determination mustered. He was going to be the person. Then before he knew what had happened he was cursing and denying Jesus. What did it? What pushed him over the edge? Was he overwhelmed? Was he out of his depth? Peter, a fisherman, not rich, stood in the palace of Caiaphas, elegant home of the richest family in the country. He had followed Jesus —a hard life—and from that he had passed to the luxury of this high priest's palace. Was he dazzled? Was he dumbfounded by the splendour? Was he breathless at the luxury? Did the contrast with all that he had known unnerve him? We don't know. But we do know that surroundings sometimes have affected us. When suddenly we are transplanted from our humble origins to wealth and position, we have been surprised very quickly into forgetting whose we are and whom we serve. I have seen it happen in Africa when students went from the rather meagre secondary schools into the well-endowed university with the whole of the grant for the session given to them in the first week. Yes, a new environment can do that.

Or was he just scared? Frightened at what would happen to him if he were arrested too? Did it suddenly dawn on him, 'They could do with me what they are doing with him'? We don't know, but we do know that others have refused to identify with Jesus because they were afraid of what was going to happen to them.

Or was it a sense of isolation? Was he cowed? He was there in that council of 70 or 71 of the most rich, most learned, most influential, most religious men in the nation, all down on Jesus. Views were being bandied about the fire by the servants. These people ought to know, he must have thought. They seemed unanimous. They couldn't all be wrong. Perhaps he thought, 'I'd better play it safe and go along.' Was it the majority that cowed him? We can't be sure, but we know that majority opinion affects others; that when they are in the minority and others seem better educated, better informed, more experienced—and when others disparage Jesus Christ—they play it safe.

Or was it shame? Jesus that night looked pretty haggard. He was having a rough time. His hands were tied; perhaps his feet were tied too. His power seemed to have gone. He had nothing to say. He was speechless. He wasn't saying anything. He was so weak and seemed so ineffective. Perhaps Peter thought, 'Can't be the same man. Have I made a mistake? Is he just human with less courage and less sense than even me tonight?' Was it disillusionment that made him turn his coat? It may not have been disillusionment for him, but it has been for others. In certain circumstances everything associated with Jesus sometimes seems so weak and unattractive and ineffectual that we don't want to be associated with him any more, and we disclaim the connection by deed or by default.

Or was it something more subtle? There was a maid in the story, a girl. Did she have a pretty face, a shapely figure? Was she the kind who set the blood tingling in his veins? Did he suddenly become infatuated so that everything else suddenly became unimportant? Did it even become important that he not be a follower of Jesus when Jesus had such high moral standards? Was it this that sprang the trap on him? We don't know, but we do know that such a temptation has caused others suddenly to forget that they were Christians.

Or was it just prevarication? Did he mean to play for time and own up later? Was he thinking, 'If I stay around now, perhaps I will be able to help later?' We have been guessing. We don't know, but we are guessing within the probabilities of the case. The Bible doesn't satisfy our curiosity. Why? In the end it is enough that he refused to identify with Jesus, whatever was the reason or the excuse. It was wrong, terribly wrong for him to do this. Whatever sprang the trap, he shouldn't have been near it and should have been wary enough to avoid it. The whole point of the story is that there is *never* any reason for any man who knows Jesus Christ to refuse to be identified with him. The reason is not dealt with, because there is never any valid reason. A denial is never excusable or justifiable.

The Pain of Entrapment

The cock crew. Peter had three times denied, and he was caught in the trap just as Jesus had said. Again Jesus was right about him, and he was wrong. He broke down and wept bitterly. How helpless he felt, and how helpless he was. Many of us—many men and women who have thought hardly of Peter— have never come near to him for depth. We have denied Jesus, but have never wept for it. Henry Drummond said about this verse, 'Let this silence forever those who disparage emotion in religion. Religion without emotion is religion without reflection.' If we have never wept before God, it is because our thinking is too shallow or non-existent.

Peter's story, however, ends with a cleansing experience. The sequel to his denial shows us the hope-

fulness of the situation. Judas died before he saw the
Cross, but Peter tells us that he was an eyewitness of
Jesus' suffering (I Peter 5:1). He didn't run away
even then, and the two disciples we know viewed the
Cross were Peter and John. When Jesus rose from
the dead—what a wonderful story it is—he said to
the women, 'Go and tell my disciples *and* Peter.'
And then Jesus himself came to Peter by the lake—
again a wonderful story—where with the most delicate communication anywhere in the Bible he recreated a scene Peter had known before. Without
words he was saying, 'Are you back on course,
Peter?' At the beginning of his ministry there had
been that scene on the lake already mentioned, when
the men had toiled all night and caught nothing.
Now at the end Jesus just recreated the scene, and
Peter began to respond. He leapt out of that boat and
splashed ashore because he said, 'That's the Lord!'
and he wanted to be there. His denial had been terrible, but his denial was not the end. There he knelt in
front of the Saviour, and in that delicate Eastern way
Jesus gives Peter three opportunities to affirm him
and to wipe out each of the times he had denied him.
'Do you love me, Peter?' 'Lord, you know that I do.'
'Do you love me, Peter?' 'Lord, you know that I do.'
And a third time. Then Jesus restored Peter to feed
his sheep, to feed his lambs, to become the boldest of
the apostles.

What does it all say to us? What are the pressures
that make us blow cold rather than hot as far as Jesus
is concerned? That make us refuse identification,
play down our 'Christianness' in our home, at

work, or in our leisure pursuits? Basically, it comes down to our self-confidence, our attempts to make it on our own and our discovery that these get us into compromising situations.

Some of us have been caught in the same trap as Peter, playing down our identification with Jesus for the same or less noticeable reasons. Pray God that we may be cut to the heart by the conviction that comes from looking in the face of the disappointed Christ, the conviction that leads on to repentance and regret before the day is out. The Cross where Jesus died is the antidote to our unwarranted self-confidence.

I have a great deal of trouble with the way in which Christians are using the word 'self' these days: self-esteem, self-confidence, self-worth. There may be something in it, but I am happy with only two words hyphenated with 'self': one is self-control, the other is self-denial. I think that I am nearer the New Testament than modern psychologists are. There is a place for confidence, but our confidence has to be in God. Our confidence has to be in our identification with Christ: 'I can do everything through him who gives me strength' (Phil. 4:13). Our confidence has to be in the fact that Jesus is in us so that we say with Paul: 'I have been crucified with Christ and I no longer live, but Christ lives in me' (Gal. 2:20). We have to say: 'God forbid that I should boast save in the Cross of Christ my God.' We can have confidence, but not in ourselves. The confidence that we have is in the Christ who is in us, who enables us, who strengthens us and makes us adequate for every situation which confronts us. As we view Peter and see the destruction of his own confidence, his boastfulness, his pride, we come ourselves to the foot of that Cross to discover how we can find strength, not in ourselves, but in him who loved us and gave himself for us.

CHAPTER 9

GAMBLING FOR THE GARMENTS

'And they crucified him. Dividing up his clothes, they cast lots to see what each would get' (Mark 15:24). Of all the episodes in the drama of the Cross, we tend to skip most quickly over this one. Its concreteness repels us: the rough, weathered wood of the upright post against his bleeding back; the iron nails tearing through flesh; the jarring of the body as the soldiers pull the ropes, heaving the cross piece up one notch at a time; death coming slowly by asphyxia, hunger, thirst; black carrion birds circling closer as the soldiers—on duty until death to prevent friends from rescuing the prisoner —throw dice to divide his garments. It is not an attractive picture. We would like to shut our eyes and believe that men do not behave that way, that this was an exception rather than the rule. 'A decent man would have to be very drunk indeed,' suggests Lloyd C. Douglas in *The Robe*, 'to exhibit such callous unconcern in this circumstance.' Somehow it is safer to think about the more abstract sins—the greed of Judas, the envy of the chief priests, the neutrality of Pilate, the indifference of the crowd—than to pause too long over the casual brutality and callousness of the soldiers.

It is not an attractive picture, but for that very

reason it may do us good to think for a moment about the soldiers gambling for the garments. All four Evangelists record the episode, but John adds additional details and refers to the fulfilment of the Messianic prophecy in Psalm 22:18.

> When the soldiers crucified Jesus, they took his clothes, dividing them into four shares, one for each of them, with the undergarment remaining. This garment was seamless, woven in one piece from top to bottom. 'Let's not tear it,' they said to one another. 'Let's decide by lot who will get it.' This happened that the Scripture might be fulfilled which said, 'They divided my garments among them and cast lots for my clothing.' So this is what the soldiers did (John 19:23, 24).

According to Roman custom the executioners could claim the possessions of the prisoner; thus after nailing Jesus to the crosspiece and hoisting him into position on the upright post, they settled down to divide his clothing while they waited for death. During the time of Jesus a Jew's clothing would have consisted of a headdress, shoes, a linen undergarment or girdle, a coat or tunic which hung down below the knees, and an outer garment or cloak. After the soldiers had divided the headdress, shoes, girdle, and cloak among themselves, the coat remained. Most coats were cut out and sewn together, but the more valuable were made of woven wool all in one piece. Just such a seamless coat Jesus had, and the soldiers decided to draw lots for it rather than tearing it into four pieces. It was a practical move. After all, it was a good coat. With little more than the occasional glance at Jesus to see that everything was proceeding as it should, they occupied themselves with the business at hand—gambling for his garments.

They weren't a particularly evil lot, as soldiers go. They were just following orders, doing their job as best they could, and exercising their prerogative of claiming the prisoner's possessions. It wasn't much compensation for drawing a bad assignment, but they took what they could get. Such an understanding of the soldiers is possible until they are viewed in the mirror of the Cross, which shows up evil for what it is. In the first instance the callousness of the soldiers crucified Jesus. Moreover, the men who inflicted the pain of crucifixion with hardly a thought and then turned callously to dividing the clothes of the victim belong to a large tribe whose clans, wherever profit is made from death, still crucify Jesus today.

Dividends from Death

The funeral undertaker's is not a much appreciated occupation. The butt of macabre jokes and the subject of sarcasm in such novels as Evelyn Waugh's *The Loved One*, he trades on death, and we hide our distaste behind our humour. The abuse of this occupation, however, fares no worse than the legacy hunters of this world who also divide the profits of

death. Where there is a will, a solicitor once re-
marked, there are relatives. Breath hardly leaves the
body of the deceased before dividing the remains
preoccupies those remaining. Often bitterness,
quarrelling, lawsuits, even estrangements form the
real legacy inherited by those who hope to profit
from what the dead have no more use for. Are not
such people blood brothers of the men who
crucified Jesus and divided his garments among
them, casting lots for them to decide what each
should take? How callous they were, dividing his
garments while his mother and best friend stood
watching. How blind they were. When we die we
take nothing out of this world. The soldiers could
see that illustrated graphically as Jesus hung there on
the Cross, yet while they grasped his garments, they
could not grasp the truth.

What about us? When we stand to gain dividends
from death, do we act as blindly and callously as the
soldiers gambling for the garments? Are we miserly?
selfish? Do we share, or do we hoard and display and
spend? God deliver us from hunting the dividends of
death. God help us so to order our affairs that there
is little to squabble about. Jesus had only his clothes
to leave; all the rest he spent for men when alive.

Gain from Grief

Crucifixion is one of the most cruel forms of execution. Used throughout the empire by Rome for its
enemies, it was considered too cruel, hence not per-
missible, for a Roman citizen. While all capital

punishment is cruel, the Jews used the death penalty sparingly and mitigated the suffering of their executions as much as possible. The typical Hebrew execution—death by stoning—happened after the prisoner had been thrown backwards from a cliff in order to break his back or stun him from the fall. Only then were stones to be thrown, and the first was to be aimed at the heart. When the Romans brought in crucifixion with its long, lingering death as their method of capital punishment, according to the Talmud, the Jews took steps to lighten the suffering of the victim. Jewish law required that a mounted guard be placed at the execution site with relays so that the authorities could stop the proceedings at any moment if they so wished. The condemned man was also given an obligatory hypnotic drink, made of incense or myrrh dissolved in wine or vinegar, to dull the pain. This was the 'sponge with wine and vinegar' (Mark 15:36) offered to Jesus but refused by him.

While some did what they could to soften the suffering of Jesus on the Cross, the Roman soldiers callously turned their backs on this most horrible of capital punishments and divided the garments with blatant insensitivity to the groans of pain within earshot. They were ready to make gains from grief even if the price was terrible suffering and pain.

Such insensitivity has not been confined to Roman soldiers. Gain from grief happens in business too. Through the centuries of slavery, peasantry, child labour, union breaking, migrant workers, and international corporations trading in Third World countries, the wealthy have gained from

exploiting the labour of the poor. 'Look! The wages
you failed to pay the workmen who mowed your
fields are crying out against you. The cries of the
harvesters have reached the ears of the Lord Almighty. You have lived on earth in luxury and self-
indulgence. You have fattened yourselves in the day
of slaughter. You have condemned and murdered
innocent men, who were opposing you' (James 5:4–
6). How much money has been made at the cost of
grief in workmen who have worked as slaves or at a
wage not much better? John Ruskin once wrote,

> Yes, if the veil could be lifted not only
> from your thoughts, but from your
> human sight, you would see—the angels
> do see—on those gay white dresses of
> yours strange dark spots, spots of the in-
> extinguishable red that all the seas cannot
> wash away: yes and among the pleasant
> flowers that crown your fair heads and
> glow on your wreathed hair, you would
> see that one weed was always twisted
> which no one thought of—the grass that
> grows on graves.

How do we get our money? How are our invest-
ments handled? Formerly there was a scandal that
the Church was drawing rents from properties used
for prostitution. Do we gain from grief like the soldiers who gambled for the garments?

Clothes from the Crucified

As the Roman soldiers got on with collecting the benefits from the crucified, they gave little notice to the Cross. They took the clothing of Jesus, but from himself they took nothing. They were satisfied with his physical possessions, but they ignored his principles. There are many so-called Christians in this clan who collect what they can from Christ without any sense of what it cost or what its inner principle is. 'If anyone would come after me, he must deny himself and take up his cross daily and follow me' Jesus had said (Luke 9:23); yet denying the Cross, some have taken up the trappings of Christianity without following Jesus. Some have conformed for the sake of an education. Now they have the fine clothes of learning and all that goes with it, but these gains are no better than the garments that the soldiers got and wore. Some have conformed for the cloaks of social esteem, for the sake of the company that they meet, for their fine wives, or for the gilt edge on their certificate of social respectability. Others just like the comfort and the aura of credit and self-esteem gained from attending a service once a week. Like the soldiers gambling for their garments, members of this clan collect clothes from the crucified, but ignore the Cross.

Righteousness from the Wronged

There is another clan that benefits from the Cross in a way that was intended. Members of this clan dis-

cover that their 'righteousness is as filthy rags'
(Isaiah 64:6) and have exchanged their rags for the
wedding garments that the Cross provided.

> Jesus, thy blood and righteousness
> My beauty are, my glorious dress,
> Midst flaming worlds, in these arrayed,
> With joy shall I lift up my head.
> (Nicholas Zinzendorf)

Members of this clan have exchanged perquisites for
a Person, clothes for character, style for sacrifice,
fashion for faith. Dressed not in the seamless garment gambled over by the soldiers, but in the wedding garments of Jesus' parable, they joyfully enter
the wedding banquet prepared by God himself for
those who love him.

CHAPTER 10

JOSEPH OF ARIMATHEA

That other player in the Crucifixion scene, Joseph of Arimathea, possesses the distinction of having certified that Jesus was dead. He fixed the signature on the death certificate of the Son of God. His part in the drama of the Cross is a sad, even pathetic, episode briefly played and quickly forgotten. Although all four Evangelists record his story, Joseph is mentioned neither before nor after this event. When Paul is preaching later in Pisidian Antioch, he simply says that 'the Jews' took Jesus down from the Cross and laid him in a tomb (Acts 13:29). Even his tomb was forgotten for centuries.

According to the apocryphal *Gospel of Nicodemus* and later legend, Joseph founded a Christian community in his home town of Lydda and then at the suggestion of St Philip in AD 63 sailed to England bearing the chalice or holy grail used at the Last Supper. There he founded the first church in the British Isles at Glastonbury, where he died. The Western Church celebrates his feast day on March 17th, but we know little about him for sure beyond what the four Evangelists tell us about him, and the brief part that he played in the drama of the Cross.

His Outstanding Career

The Evangelists unanimously agree on his career. Matthew tells us that he was a rich man. Mark and Luke mention that he was a ruler, a member of the Sanhedrin, or council of 70, and thus he was one of the most distinguished men in all Jewry. Mark adds that he was a prominent or respected member, and Luke calls him a good and upright or righteous man. According to Mark he 'was himself waiting for the kingdom of God' (Mark 15:43). Joseph of Arimathea was a religious man, devoutly hoping for the deliverance of Israel through the Messiah. It is a fine portrait. The Evangelists are very courteous in their sketching of him.

His Obscure Conversion

From this description one might expect him to have been drawn to Jesus, and he was. In his own heart he had admitted the truth of Jesus' claim to be the Messiah, the initiator of the Kingdom of God. Matthew says 'he had himself become a disciple of Jesus' (Matt. 27:57). Yet he did not come out into the open. Says John, 'Now Joseph was a disciple of Jesus, but secretly because he feared the Jews' (John 19:38). Like Nicodemus, his colleague in the Sanhedrin who came to Jesus at night (John 3), Joseph of Arimathea has been called a 'twilight disciple' or a 'disciple in the dark', for in our story he did nothing until darkness had fallen.

Why did Joseph keep his conversion secret? As a

member of the ruling council he had much to lose and much to conserve. He had position, influence, power, and he had to decide how best to use it. Should he have resigned from his position, forsaken all, and joined the group of disciples that followed Jesus from place to place? After all, Jesus had said, 'any of you who does not give up everything he has cannot be my disciple' (Luke 14:33). Any responsible ruler, however, works to preserve the peace and stability of society, and that often means supporting the status quo instead of backing a revolutionary leader. Should he have remained in the Sanhedrin and proclaimed his discipleship publicly, incurring the certain wrath of his colleagues and accepting whatever consequences followed? Or should he have said nothing openly but worked behind the scenes to persuade his colleagues to moderate their hostility toward Jesus? In which way could he have the most influence—do the most good for Jesus and the Jews?

If we could answer that question for Joseph of Arimathea, we could answer it for ourselves, for there are many like him today—people in the spotlight of public life, people in positions of authority on every level of society, people who feel the tension between official duty and religious commitment. What do we do when we see Christ crucified in racial prejudice, economic injustice, or political corruption? How do we combat evil when the whole system is corrupt and injustice reigns as official policy? It is not an easy answer for us or for Joseph.

Whether out of fear of his colleagues or out of genuine belief that he could effect change behind the scenes, Joseph decided to remain silent. It wasn't an easy course. As he stood on the edge of the crowd listening to Jesus in the temple, he silently accepted Jesus as the Messiah; yet as he sat with the chief priests in the Sanhedrin, he silently acquiesced in their condemnation of this troublesome prophet from Nazareth. This internal civil war finally involved him in an opposition from which he could not escape. The chief priests arrested Jesus and brought him before the Sanhedrin to try him for blasphemy. Even here, however, we do not know for sure what Joseph of Arimathea did. According to Luke's account Joseph 'had not consented to their decision and action' (Luke 23:51); yet according to Mark's description of the trial before the Sanhedrin, 'they all condemned him as worthy of death' (Mark 14:64). Did he prudently absent himself from the Sanhedrin that night? Or did he attend but abstain from voting, neither condemning the proceedings nor taking part in the condemnation of Christ, remaining silent to the end?

His Overdue Courage

It is easy to condemn Joseph for the failures of secret discipleship. Jesus himself said, 'If anyone is ashamed of me and my words, the Son of Man will be ashamed of him when he comes in his glory and in the glory of the Father and of the holy angels' (Luke 9:26). Yet the story of Joseph doesn't end here. When Joseph realised that the opposition inevitably arising from secret discipleship had led to the Cross, he discovered his overdue courage. Mark says that Joseph went 'boldly' to Pilate and asked for the body, and he uses a word that in the original means 'to dare', 'to be brave enough', 'to summon up courage'. Why did Joseph's action require courage?

Jewish law required the body of an executed man to be buried before night. 'If a man guilty of a capital offence is put to death and his body is hung on a tree, you must not leave his body on the tree overnight. Be sure to bury him that same day, because anyone who is hung on a tree is under God's curse' (Deut. 21:22, 23). According to Roman custom, however, the bodies of the crucified would be left to decay on the cross and would eventually be cast out as refuse, a prey to carrion birds and beasts. Roman law did allow relatives to claim the body for a price and give it a decent burial, but Joseph was no relative. Although he was wealthy enough to offer Pilate his price, he could claim no kinship with Jesus. His request meant coming out into the open. It meant declaring publicly that he was a disciple.

Nightfall was approaching. John had taken Mary into the city; Peter had denied Jesus; the other disciples had scattered. Someone had to do something. Rich and comfortable as he was, he no doubt shrank from the inevitable trouble and dangers of open discipleship, yet he disregarded his angry colleagues and faced Pilate alone. And that took courage.

Read superficially, the rest of the narrative tells a pathetic story. Accompanied by Nicodemus, that other secret disciple of Jesus, Joseph took the body down from the cross and prepared it for burial. He brought a shroud, and Nicodemus brought a mixture of myrrh and aloes weighing 75 pounds, far more spices than were necessary. Was Nicodemus, too, trying to make up for lost opportunities? Together they wrapped Jesus' body with the spices and strips of linen and laid it in Joseph's own new tomb. Together they performed the last offices for the lacerated body and then rolled a stone against the door of the tomb. It was the only thing left to do. Their discipleship had begun, not at the eleventh hour like that of the servants in Jesus' parable, but at five minutes after midnight—too late to bring any joy to Jesus, too late to bring any joy to themselves. It is always pathetic to be too late, especially in death, to be ready only after life has gone, to realise what could have been after the opportunity has passed. This is Joseph's word to the world. He says, in effect, don't be like me.

His Open Consolation

Little did Joseph know, as the stone settled into place with a terrible, grating finality, that the finality was deceptive. No gravestone could withstand the power of the Son of God. Likewise, no stone is ever final when the living power of the resurrected Christ rolls back the stone and steps into our lives. Failures, disappointments, defeats, frustrations, like sealed gravestones may mar the garden of Golgotha, yet God never notices stones. Earth's finalities do not bind him. In sorrow we may seal a stone against some portion of our past, yet God has many ways of opening tombs and liberating us.

Little did Joseph know, as he turned his back on the tomb, his heart as heavy as that gravestone, that in 36 hours all his work would be unnecessary. The linen shroud would be neatly folded inside the tomb, the stone would be rolled away, the spices of Nicodemus and those brought by Mary Magdalene, Mary the mother of James, and Salome would be irrelevant. What a relief! The shroud, the spices, the tomb mattered little; but the little he had done, seemingly too late, was not too late. Jesus had risen, and Jesus knew who had cared for him in those final black hours of darkness. Like Joseph, we too may have wasted long years and time and energy, but it is never too late in this life with Christ. The Risen One stands ready to receive whoever comes to him, whether the thief on the cross or Joseph of Arimathea.

CHAPTER 11

RESURRECTION IN THE CAPITAL CITY

This scene opens on Saturday night, some time after six o'clock. By Jewish custom the Sabbath was over and weekday activities could be resumed. The principal characters who had engineered the Crucifixion met again at Pilate's residence: they were the chief priests who did not believe in resurrection, the Pharisees who did, and Pilate who was anxious to be finished with the whole business and was probably irritated at being approached at all. 'Sir,' they said with mock humility, 'we remember that while he was still alive that deceiver said, "After three days I will rise again." So give the order for the tomb to be made secure until the third day. Otherwise, his disciples may come and steal the body and tell the people that he has been raised from the dead. This last deception will be worse than the first' (Matt. 27:63, 64).

It is a revealing speech!

The thought of Jesus' rising again or even of there being any talk of his having risen had clearly frightened the authorities. Their creed said 'Dead men don't talk', and for their purpose, resurrection or anything after death would be decidedly inconvenient, even disastrous. Their deed might yet recoil on their heads, and that would threaten the dearest thing in the world to them—their power. Thus, even though it meant unseemly haste after the Sabbath— just as the Crucifixion had meant unseemly haste before the Sabbath—something had to be done about it.

The Resurrection Challenges Human Authority

Ordinarily, this deputation would not have been necessary, for as the death sentence was Roman responsibility, what happened to the body was also Roman responsibility. Unfortunately, one of their own number had stepped out of line and complicated matters. Joseph of Arimathea, a wealthy and respected member of their parliament, seeing in the Cross what official diplomacy had led to, had finished with keeping quiet and toeing the line, had gone 'boldly', asked for the body, and put it in his own private tomb. That had complicated matters and had made this deputation to the governor necessary to see that due security precautions were taken. It always threatens unscrupulous authorities when one of their own number steps out of line and does the right thing or even the decent thing; however, Caiaphas was not the man to be thwarted by any pious-minded or sensitive-conscienced man like Joseph. Things could be taken care of.

Notice their approach. It was based on the conviction that if a falsehood is repeated often enough, people will come to believe it—the fundamental idea behind all unethical propaganda. 'That liar' they called Jesus. Such falsehood seems to us incredible, but we should not be incredulous. Officialdom is quite capable of such perverted insinuations if they suit the purpose. Then to keep up the myth, they suggested that the disciples might steal the body and then tell another lie that 'he had been raised from the dead'. Where did they get this idea? Surely they got it from their own devious, corrupt minds. This is what they would have done in the circumstances, and perhaps Judas made them think that even the disciples of Jesus would not stop at resorting to the same tactics. It would have the added value, of course, that it fuelled the propaganda that this was a dangerous and unscrupulous movement; and in any case it had to be clear that the government could do no wrong.

Their last sentence shows acute perception: 'This last deception will be worse than the first.' Now the first lie, according to them, was that Jesus was the Son of God (Matt. 26:63–66). Without investigating this claim of Jesus, they shouted that it was blasphemy and condemned him out of hand, even ignoring the prescribed trial procedures for cases of blasphemy. They were not ready to consider whether or not it was true, so they called it a lie and him a liar— all very impressive, especially if, like the high priest, one goes into a fit of indignation, tearing clothes and shouting. Now, however, they saw that any suggestion that Jesus had been raised from the dead would be even more difficult to deal with because, of course, apart from its own significance, the Resurrection would make the first 'lie' a truth also. Jesus really would be the Son of God, for his Resurrection would prove his identity. That is why to them the last lie would be even worse than the first. It would cause trouble for them with their bosses and with the people, and even more importantly, if there were a Resurrection, they would be called to account after death for what they had done. How clearly these unscrupulous men grasped the implications of the Resurrection.

The Resurrection Defies Human Security

That, then, was their pretty speech, laying bare the kind of men they were. How did Pilate react? He quickly gave them the permission they wanted. 'Take a guard,' Pilate answered. 'Go, make the tomb as secure as you know how' (Matt. 27:65). There is a touch of sarcasm here. 'Go, make the tomb as secure as you know how.' That is all that is open to authorities, especially corrupt authorities. Make it as sure as you can. Unfortunately for them, it was the one inside the grave who could say, 'All authority in heaven and on earth has been given to me' (Matt. 28:18). As long as that is true, no one can bury the truth nor imprison justice nor contain love. One can only try to make it as sure as he can, and that is what they did. They used a large stone, a carefully placed official seal, and a guard of soldiers. A stone, a seal, and some sentries: they manipulated the physical conditions, the legal trappings, and the armed militia. That was as secure as they could make it.

It didn't do much good. They were pitting themselves against God and the ultimate nature of things.

We, too, would like to have things the way we want them, and sometimes men imagine that they can carry it off if they can control the law, the army, and the physical conditions. Sooner or later, however, reality asserts itself. One can tamper only temporarily with natural law and moral law. The pendulum swings back inevitably, and in their case it swung back immediately. Before dawn, the seal was broken; the stone was rolled back; the soldiers were scattered with astonishment; and Jesus Christ rose from death. Nowhere are we told precisely what happened. If anyone witnessed the actual event, it was the soldiers. Matthew says, 'Some of the guards went into the city and reported to the chief priests everything that had happened' (Matt. 28:11). Their report, however, was highly dangerous material to the chief priests; they called a meeting with a select few of the elders and immediately suppressed the story. The narrative gives no hint of their being impressed or their beginning to think that they had been wrong about Jesus. Like all corrupt officials they were sticking to their story and clinging to their power. By the time their dawn meeting broke up, they had the whole thing worked out and everything taken care of.

First they found a large sum of money to bribe the soldiers. It probably provided enough for them to retire and set up in a business or a farm somewhere as they had always dreamed, for the bribe accomplished its purpose and kept them in line. The story they were primed to tell had two points: first, the disciples came during the night and stole the body; and second, this happened while they dozed off to sleep for a bit. Apparently the inconsistency of the two halves did not occur to them—if they were asleep, how did they know that the body had been stolen or who had done it? We need not be surprised at this, however, for such inconsistent explanations are well known in politics, even today, and the corroboration of them kept inaccessible under the guise of security or privilege.

The Resurrection Outwits Human Mendacity

One thing, however, did get through—the body was missing and could not be produced. That the authorities did not produce it showed that they had not removed it. That the disciples did not steal it is clear from the complete confidence with which they went out to live and die in the faith that Jesus was risen. That no one else produced the body proves that no one could, for the incentives to do so were irresistible. However you look at it, it always comes back to the word of the young man at the grave—'He is not here'—and no other reason than the one he gave adequately explains its disappearance—'He has risen, just as he said' (Matt. 28:6).

The authorities, however, could not accept that explanation. They stuck to the story that they had bribed the guards to tell. The soldiers took a risk in repeating their tale; it could have led to their being court-martialled. The priests had foreseen this possible objection and had said in advance, 'If this report gets to the governor, we will satisfy him and keep you out of trouble' (Matt. 28:14). They could

take care of Pilate. They had managed him pretty
well in the matter of the Crucifixion, and now, of
course, they had another trump card in their hand—
the Crucifixion itself. Men like the chief priests get
others like Pilate involved deeply and then threaten
them with exposure if they show signs of trying to
pull out and go straight. Apparently they had no
trouble with Pilate; they had tied his hands. The
guards also kept their part of the bargain according
to Matthew: 'So the soldiers took the money and did
as they were instructed. And this story has been
widely circulated among the Jews to this very day'
(Matt. 28:15). If any of them had been converted, we
would have heard the story of that night in the garden. What we know must have leaked from the
council itself in an indirect way, for it was just
enough to give us the facts of the deception without
the details that were hushed up.

Once Jesus had told the story of a rich man in hell
who wanted someone to go and warn his five
brothers about the terrors of hell. Jesus said that it
would be no use. If men do not change with the truth
that is available to them, someone rising from the
dead and telling them would not make any difference. How right he was! In his own case his rising
from the dead left those who had engineered his
death on the Cross completely unchanged. It was
the same mixture as before. Lies, bribes, and political manoeuvring had crucified Jesus; and lies, bribes,
and political manoeuvring tried to discredit his Resurrection.

The Resurrection of Jesus threatens corrupt
leadership. It introduces and establishes factors that

cannot be controlled. The chief priests made it as sure as they could. Still Jesus rose. They made and executed their counter plan; still within 50 days 3,000 people had discovered Jesus to be very much alive, and the number grew rapidly thereafter, creating trouble upon trouble for these leaders. After relating the frantic attempts of the chief priests to control the Resurrection, Matthew goes on almost with a chuckle to quote Jesus, 'All authority in heaven and on earth has been given to *me*. Therefore go and make disciples of all nations ... And surely I will be with you always, to the very end of the age' (Matt. 28:18–20).

Sometimes we see justice turned back, righteousness standing afar off, and truth sadly lacking; 'whoever shuns evil becomes a prey' (Isa. 59:15). It is the Cross all over again, but the Cross is never the end. Jesus rose and all authority is invested in him. His Resurrection is the unshakable evidence that truth will ultimately triumph and justice finally be done. As the hymn 'Once to every man and nation' says,

> Though the cause of evil prosper
>   Yet 'tis truth alone is strong,
> Though her portion be the scaffold
>   And upon the throne be wrong,
> Yet that scaffold sways the future
>   And, behind the dim unknown,
> Standeth God within the shadow
>   Keeping watch above his own.

God is love, and love cannot be outwitted. The Cross and the Resurrection show us that forever.

Whose side are we on? Are we most readily identified with those who crucified Jesus for selfish ends and tried to hush up his Resurrection in order to hang on to their paltry power? What do our actions in the last year indicate as the answer to this question?

Or are we identified with the other bunch of hard-hearted, sceptical men and emotional women in the story? They had no more to their credit than the first lot. They found it too good to be true that Jesus, whom they had deserted, doubted, and denied, had come back loving and looking for them. He wanted to take them in hand permanently and bring out all the potential for good that was in them and put them to work for him. He recovered them from their fear and doubt and depression and worked such a radical transformation in them that they in turn went out and turned the world upside down. The same could happen to us if in penitence we believe in the Resurrection and accept the risen Jesus as the Son of God. Then we will know a new kind of power—not the ineffective power of a corrupt and selfish officialdom —but the power of the Resurrection, the power to rise again from evil and sin and unworthy conduct to integrity, truth and love.

CHAPTER 12

THE EVIDENCE THAT COULD NOT BE USED FOR A FACT THAT COULD NOT BE DENIED

Most reliable manuscripts of Mark's gospel end quite dramatically in mid-sentence. 'Trembling and bewildered,' Mark wrote, 'the women went out and fled from the tomb. They said nothing to anyone, because they were afraid ...' Why did Mark stop here? Why did he not explain the silence and fear of Mary Magdalene, Mary the mother of James, and Salome? Though Bible translators today have generally added a full stop at the end of Mark 16:8, scholars agree that it should more correctly be punctuated with some mark of incompleteness. (Verses 9–20 following are not added in the most reliable manuscripts.) So the Resurrection scene in the drama of the Cross stops abruptly here with a broken sentence.

We do know that the three women had gone to Jesus' place of burial to anoint his body with spices, only to find the great stone moved from the door and the body gone. What we don't know is how absolute was their silence afterwards. But we also know that when Christians began to preach about Jesus, they emphasised the centrality of the Resurrection, yet they never mentioned in any of their sermons the women who came at dawn to the tomb and found it empty. Twenty years later, when Paul tabulated the people to whom Jesus appeared as evidence for the Resurrection, he mentioned some not recorded in the gospels, but remained completely silent about this experience of the women.

The story was first recorded about 30 years later when Mark wrote his gospel, breaking the long silence the women had kept. 'They said nothing to anyone, because they were afraid.' Nor may we assume that their silence and Mark's reluctance to elaborate upon it even after 30 years came about because the disciples did not know. Mark uses identical words about the man healed of leprosy without any hint of their meaning absolute silence: 'See that you don't tell this to anyone. But go, show yourself to the priest' (Mark 1:44). The other gospels confirm that the woman did tell the other disciples (Luke 24:9 and John 20:2). Yet there the story stopped, and the silence started. To solve this mystery surrounding the silence of the women, let us note several points about the story.

Its Authenticity

The story reads like a vivid eyewitness account. Mark notes precisely that three women—Mary Magdalene, Mary the mother of James and Joses, and Salome—watched the Crucifixion (15:40); two of them—Mary Magdalene and Mary the mother of Joses—witnessed the burial (15:47); and then all three again were bringing spices after the Sabbath to anoint his body (16:1). He records the precise time of day—just after sunrise (16:2)—and the overheard conversation of the women as they approached the tomb—'Who will roll the stone away from the entrance of the tomb?' (16:3). The stone is mentioned three times (15:46, 16:3, and 16:4) suggesting the vivid memory of a great problem solved. He describes their alarm at the sight of the young man in white (16:5); the breathless, staccato message—Don't be afraid. He has risen! He is not here. See where they laid him. Go! Tell his disciples and Peter (16:6–7)—and their hysterical departure as they fled trembling and bewildered (16:8). The entire account has the air of a vivid eyewitness narrative.

Its Author

'As they entered the tomb, they saw a young man dressed in a white robe sitting on the right side' (Mark 16:5). The young man is often assumed to be an angel, but that assumption is not necessary or even likely. The word used here for 'young man' nowhere else in Scripture means angel. It appears only one other time in Mark's gospel at the arrest of Jesus where it has traditionally been understood to refer to Mark himself. 'A young man, wearing nothing but a linen garment, was following Jesus. When they seized him, he fled naked, leaving his garment behind' (Mark 14:51, 52). This little incident, which appears only in Mark's gospel and which adds nothing important to the narrative, has been described as 'the monogram of the painter in a dark corner of the picture.'

Neither does the white robe necessarily imply angelic garb. In Revelation the glorified believers are several times described as wearing white robes (Rev. 6:11; 7:9, 13), but the same word is also used to describe the clothing worn by the teachers of the law (Mark 12:38) and simply means a long flowing robe. Furthermore, the message of the young man to the women—'He is going ahead of you into Galilee. There you will see him, just as he told you' (Mark 16:7)—also implies that the messenger had been present in the garden before the arrest. Then Jesus had said to his disciples, 'But after I have risen, I will go ahead of you into Galilee' (Mark 14:28). All this adds up to the inference that the young man in the tomb on Resurrection morning was Mark himself. The other gospels report that the women were emotionally moved, but only Mark writes with the detail of an eyewitness and then only much later, away from Jerusalem, for an Italian readership.

Its Awkwardness

Why didn't Mark disclose his story earlier? The chief priests had spread the rumour in Jerusalem that the disciples had removed the body (Matt. 28:11–15). At least that was the story that the soldiers were telling. There was evidence that three women previously associated with Jesus and one man were at the tomb at or before dawn. Obviously their names could not be divulged, for they had no alibi for the accusation. In fact, not only that day but for much of the next 40 days the disciples were keeping a low profile. On the evening of the Resurrection 'the disciples were together, with the doors locked for fear of the Jews' (John 20:19). A week later, when Jesus appeared to Thomas, the disciples were still in the house with the doors locked (John 20:26). Only after a minimum of two weeks did they dare to depart for Galilee. This fearful approach accounts for the silence of much of the forty days between the Resurrection and the Ascension.

Its Accuracy

What exactly was the evidence of the women? That Jesus had risen? No. Not primarily. Their evidence verified that the tomb was empty. Why was it suppressed? No one needed it. The guards were saying it. Anyone could check it for himself, as did Peter and John, and verify it in five minutes' walk to the garden. When the apostles began to preach about the Resurrection on the day of Pentecost, there was no need to argue. The empty tomb was an accepted fact.

Now that is great evidence. Sceptics have often tried to explain it but have never explained it away. Some have tried to discredit the story by pointing to the inconsistencies in the gospel accounts of the women's story—Matthew says an angel spoke to the women, John says two angels, Luke says two men, and Mark says a young man—but these conflicting details could easily have arisen from the natural hysteria and fear of the three women each telling the story. On the important points—the empty tomb and the risen Jesus—they all agree. Others have argued that the women went to the wrong tomb. Mary Magdalene and Mary the mother of Joses, however, did see where he was buried (Mark 15:47). It is not likely that they both would have mistaken such an important matter, and at any rate the authorities could have produced the gardener to verify the correct tomb. Still others have argued that Joseph of Arimathea removed the body, but such an act is out of character for a respected and righteous religious leader. He made no disclosure of the body nor erected any shrine to honour his Lord. Neither did the authorities remove the body, for simply producing the body would have ended the argument. They would have if they could have. Nor did the disciples steal the body as the chief priests charged. Their subsequent preaching would have carried no conviction nor would any of them have died a martyr's death, as some of them did, if they were speaking of a fraud. The evidence of the women will not go away: the tomb was empty.

Even when confronted with the evidence that cannot be denied, many people do not find the truth of the Resurrection easy to accept. This is not strange, nor is it new. It is as old as the Resurrection itself. Even the disciples, those who knew Jesus best, had great difficulty in accepting the Resurrection. When Mary Magdalene believed, the other disciples scoffed: 'When they heard that Jesus was alive and that she had seen him, they did not believe it' (Mark 16:11). 'It was Mary Magdalene, Joanna, Mary the mother of James, and the others with them who told this to the apostles. But they did not believe the women, because their words seemed to them like nonsense' (Luke 24:10, 11).

Even after hearing the women's story of the empty tomb and having it verified by Peter and John, the men on the road to Emmaus were content to say in the past tense, 'we had hoped that he was the one who was going to redeem Israel' (Luke 24:21). When the men on the Emmaus road believed, the other disciples still scoffed: 'Afterward Jesus appeared in a different form to two of them while they were walking in the country. These returned and reported it to the rest; but they did not believe them either. Later Jesus appeared to the Eleven as they were eating; he rebuked them for their lack of faith and their stubborn refusal to believe those who had seen him after he had risen' (Mark 16:12–14). When the other disciples finally believed, Thomas scoffed: 'Unless I see the nail marks in his hands and put my finger where the nails were, and put my hand into his side, I will not believe it' (John 20:25). Even in the Early Church believers scoffed: 'But if it is preached that Christ has been raised from the dead, how can some of you say that there is no resurrection of the dead? If there is no resurrection of the dead, then not even Christ has been raised. And if Christ has not been raised, our preaching is useless and so is your faith' (I Cor. 15:12–14). Difficulty in believing the Resurrection is not a new thing.

Belief in the Resurrection has never been easy. The Resurrection cannot be proved absolutely; neither can it be disproved absolutely. Nevertheless, belief in the Resurrection is essential. Apostolic preaching gave it prominence and made it a condition of salvation. 'If you confess with your mouth, "Jesus is Lord," and believe in your heart that God raised him from the dead, you will be saved' (Rom. 10:9). Belief in the Resurrection is difficult, yet all of us must personally encounter the risen Jesus and must decide for ourselves whether or not to believe. Revelation comes not to the curious or to the sceptic but to the seeker.

CHAPTER 13

MARY MAGDALENE

As the post-Resurrection drama unfolded, the first person to encounter the risen Jesus and to believe was Mary Magdalene. The guards had reported the empty tomb to the chief priests, who frantically scrambled to explain away the evidence. The three women—Mary Magdalene, Mary the mother of James, and Salome—had reported the empty tomb to the disciples who scoffed because the report sounded to them like nonsense. While Peter and John ran to the tomb to verify their story and while the rest of the disciples hid behind locked doors because they feared the chief priests, Mary Magdalene wandered back to the garden in bewilderment.

Numb with grief, she had watched the Crucifixion. She had seen Jesus wince and cry out as the nails drove through his flesh. She had heard him call out for water. She had seen his body slump as he breathed his last breath. She had watched as Nicodemus and Joseph of Arimathea had lowered the body from the Cross, wrapped it with spices, and carried it to the garden tomb. Determined to add her spices to theirs, she had risen early and come to the garden, only to find the tomb open and the body gone. When she ran to tell the disciples, they had not believed her. Little wonder that she now stood crying in front of the tomb.

Mary's Devotion

We know very little about Mary Magdalene before her part in the drama of the Cross and Resurrection, aside from a passing reference to her in Luke's gospel. 'After this, Jesus travelled about from one town and village to another, proclaiming the good news of the kingdom of God. The Twelve were with him, and also some women who had been cured of evil spirits and diseases: Mary (called Magdalene) from whom seven demons had come out; Joanna the wife of Chuza, the manager of Herod's household; Susanna; and many others. These women were helping to support them out of their own means' (Luke 8:1–3).

Mary came from the town of Magdala on the Sea of Galilee, three miles from Capernaum, and she probably joined the disciples during Jesus' second mission through Galilee in the second year of his ministry. We do not know whether she was single or married, widowed or divorced. Many have speculated about the meaning of the 'seven demons'; theories include epilepsy, acute melancholia and depression, or even immorality and prostitution. The latter suggestion, although unlikely, has been kept alive by the confusion of Mary Magdalene with the unnamed prostitute who anointed the feet of Jesus with perfume (Luke 7:36–50) and with Mary of Bethany, who performed the same act of devotion (John 11:2).

Whatever the nature of the seven demons, Jesus had rescued Mary Magdalene from a physical or spiritual bondage that had held her captive and controlled her life. She was beginning to know deliverance through Jesus, and she followed him out of gratitude. Her life was now centred on his person. She couldn't do enough for him. She used her own money to help support him (Luke 8:3), following him and caring for his needs (Mark 15:41). During the Crucifixion and the burial Mary would not let Jesus out of her sight. She watched from a distance as the soldiers crucified him and the chief priests mocked him (Mark 15:40). She had heard him cry out, 'My God, my God, why have you forsaken me?' She heard him utter a loud cry and saw him breathe his last. Even then she had not deserted her watch, for she saw Joseph of Arimathea come for the body, followed him to the tomb, and saw where he laid Jesus (Mark 15:47). When the other disciples had scattered, Mary Magdalene was there.

After a sleepless and distraught Sabbath she was there again while it was still dark, now with more spices for his body. According to John's gospel she was first there at the tomb and first away with the news that the body was gone. 'She came running to Simon Peter and the other disciple, the one Jesus loved, and said, "They have taken the Lord out of the tomb, and we don't know where they have put him!"' (John 20:1). Later, as she stood before the tomb crying, she said to the two angels, 'They have taken my Lord away, and I don't know where they have put him' (John 20:13). In her grief and single-minded devotion even mistaking Jesus for the gardener, she said in her bewilderment, 'Sir, if you have carried him away, tell me where you have put him, and I will get him' (John 20:15). She excelled all the others in her attention. For two years she had followed him, supported him, loved him, depended on him, devoted her life to him; and now, distracted, weeping and bewildered, she could not find him.

Mary's Demoralisation

Jesus once made a comment on the after-effects of demon possession. 'When an evil spirit comes out of a man, it goes through arid places seeking rest and does not find it. Then it says, "I will return to the house I left." When it arrives, it finds the house swept clean and put in order. Then it goes and takes seven other spirits more wicked than itself, and they go in and live there. And the final condition of that man is worse than the first' (Luke 11:24–26). This is the only other reference in the New Testament to seven evil spirits. Whether or not it refers directly to the seven demons cast out of Mary Magdalene, it does cast light on what Mary might have gone through. An abortive experience of deliverance from depression might have left her in a worse state than at first.

There are many people like Mary Magdalene. They have known God's love, and their lives have changed dramatically. They have experienced the joy and wonder and excitement of following Jesus, and at one time they could not do enough for him in return. Like Mary they were entirely devoted. Then death or circumstances or a broken home or a broken marriage removes the centre of their life, leaving a hole so great that none can fill it. Certainties that they thought that they could count on—a Christian faith, a loving marriage, or a steady job—fall apart before their eyes. Nothing seems certain any longer. Like Mary stand-

ing helplessly by the Cross, unable to stop the soldiers or priests but compelled to witness the cruel
drama to its end, they have been made to suffer
events that they could not control. Hearts broken in
sorrow, they have struggled under the crushing
weight of loss and depression. Frustrated in their attempts to perform even a simple task like anointing
the body with spices, they have sunk into depression
so black and so heavy that they cannot carry on. Distracted, weeping and bewildered—like Mary—they
have lost the way back to Resurrection faith and life.

Mary's Deliverance

How does one grope back from depression to light
and life again? How did Mary find her way? First,
she went to the right place and spoke to the right
people. She was there where she had last seen Jesus.
Three times she went back to the tomb, even when
everyone else had given up. She spoke to the disciples and told them her grief about the missing body.
She asked the two angels where he was, and then she
asked Jesus.

What do we do when we suffer from deep depression? I have a friend who went through a tragic divorce. He wants to believe but never quite makes it.
He avoids Christians and only seldom comes to
church. He almost seems to need his loss to feed on
and does not really want help to get over it. But not
Mary! Instead of staying at home alone without
talking to anyone, instead of nursing her grief in isolation, or making complaint in the wrong ears, Mary

Magdalene went to the right place and kept asking the right questions to the right people.

Secondly, Mary realised Christ's personal knowledge of and care for her. She did not find him; he found her. Like Mary we may have lost our way in doubt, loss, depression, or bewilderment. We may not know where to begin looking, or we may not even want to look; but Jesus is already there in our depression, looking for us and calling us by name.

> Calling, calling, Jesus is calling,
>   Calling you by your name.
> Back through the avenues of wandering
>   Child of mine come home again.

In the Gorbals in Glasgow a social worker was taking a survey in the slums. He knocked on a door, and when a woman answered, he asked how many people lived in the house. The woman replied, 'There's Jimmy and Mary and Sadie and Bobby—' 'Just give me the numbers,' the social worker interrupted. The woman replied, 'There are no numbers in this house. They are all names to me.' Likewise we are all names to God. Jesus tenderly asked why Mary was crying and then called her by name. Only then did she recognise him.

Thirdly, Mary had to learn what was and what was not possible. When she recognised Jesus, she cried, 'Rabboni!' which means teacher, and joyfully clung to him. Her form of address suggests Mary's desire to resume the old attitude and relationship to Jesus. She wanted to return to the way things had been before Jesus had died, caring for him, providing for his needs out of her wealth, following him through the dusty towns and villages of Galilee. Now she could shut out the nightmare of the last three days. Everything would be as it had been before. But Jesus gently released her hands and said, 'Do not hold on to me, for I have not yet returned to the Father' (John 20:17). Jesus was no longer a man in the flesh. He had a resurrected body. They would have a new relationship now. In the same way for us, past relationships or experiences sometimes cannot be revived after a loss. No matter how much we may desire to, we cannot return to the same place twice. Loss of a colleague, the death of a friend, the break-up of a marriage all change our thinking, our attitudes and our relationships. We, like Mary, have to discover what is and what is not possible on the other side of despair.

Fourthly, Mary had to rid herself of her old view of God. After his Resurrection 'Jesus appeared in a different form' (Mark 16:12) to the disciples on the road to Emmaus, and they could not recognise him. Neither could Mary. 'She turned around and saw Jesus standing there, but she did not realise that it was Jesus' (John 20:14). Face to face with the risen Jesus, Mary mistook him for the gardener because she was looking for a dead human body rather than a resurrected body. In the same way we often look for God in one form; and when he comes to us in another, we do not recognise him and think that we have been left alone in our despair. We have stereotyped, set ideas about God. We expect him to manifest himself by bringing us material prosperity or physical healing or immunity from disaster. When we cannot find him in that form, we fall into despair. Next time we are sure that God has deserted us, let us stop looking for him to do what he has never promised and discover that he has been with us all the time in a different form. Only we may have thought that he was the gardener. The God that we discover when we are sure that no one is there will be the true God.

Finally, Mary had to trust in the new unique relationship with God through Christ. When speaking of the Father, Jesus had always said *my* Father, never *our* Father. His sonship was unique. Now he was extending that unique sonship to Mary and to the disciples and to all who would believe. 'Go instead to my brothers and tell them, "I am returning to my Father and your Father, to my God and your God"' (John 20:17).

He is my Father and also your Father, my God and also your God. The Cross and the Resurrection changed forever our relationship with God and made us adopted children in the unique family of God. 'You received the Spirit of sonship. And by him we cry, "*Abba*, Father." The Spirit himself testifies with our spirit that we are God's children. Now if we are children, then we are heirs—heirs of God and co-heirs with Christ, if indeed we share in his sufferings in order that we may also share in his glory' (Rom. 8:15–17). May we, like Mary, come into that adopted family with confidence, believing that God is our Father, that he loves us, and that his love never changes. Only then can we discover the new relationships, define the new possibilities, and find the God who is there on the other side of our depression and doubt.

CHAPTER 14

THOMAS

Thomas steps on stage to play his part in the drama of the Cross with a character label firmly attached. The epithet 'doubting Thomas' has come to stand for the pessimist who always attaches the worst possible interpretation to events, or for the sceptic who refuses to believe anything good without visible, tangible proof. In part Thomas deserves his label, but he also shows us, in his confrontation with the risen Christ, the way through doubt to faith.

Faith and Temperament

Apart from the mention of his name in the list of disciples called by Jesus, the first appearance of Thomas in the gospels comes in the story of the raising of Lazarus. When Jesus received the message from Mary and Martha that Lazarus was sick, he told his disciples that he was returning to Judaea. '"But Rabbi," they said, "a short while ago the Jews tried to stone you, and yet you are going back there?"' (John 11:8). When no amount of protest could persuade Jesus that the journey to Bethany would be foolhardy, perhaps even fatal, Thomas with a shrug of pessimistic resignation said to the rest of the disciples, 'Let us also go, that we may die with him' (John 11:16). Thomas knew that the journey would end in failure or disaster. He was sure of that. Yet if Jesus insisted on returning, he was resigned to follow. His loyalty or courage was never in question. At issue was his pessimism, his inability to understand or even in his wildest dreams to imagine that Jesus had power over life and death. As they trudged the dusty road toward Bethany, they were not marching toward humiliation and defeat as he imagined; instead they were about to witness the greatest demonstration yet of God's power—the miraculous resurrection of Lazarus. Even so, Thomas knew that the plan was doomed to failure. He was sure of that.

Thomas displays the same pessimism during his second appearance in the gospels at the Last Supper. Jesus had just finished reassuring his disciples. 'Do not let your hearts be troubled. Trust in God; trust also in me. In my Father's house are many rooms; if it were not so, I would have told you. I am going there to prepare a place for you. And if I go and prepare a place for you, I will come back and take you to be with me that you also may be where I am. You know the way to the place where I am going' (John 14:1–4). With his characteristic down-to-earth bluntness Thomas interrupted Jesus, 'Lord, we don't know where you are going, so how can we know the way?' (John 14:5). His tone of voice expresses not bewilderment or anxiety, but pessimism. 'Come off it,' we hear him say. 'I haven't yet seen the slightest trace of the Father's house. I have no idea where you are going. I don't know the way. If you are going to die now, we might as well die too.' No amount of reassurance from Jesus could break through the wall of black pessimism that Thomas had erected around his life. No amount of encouragement could lighten the gloom inside.

Thomas's doubt had its root in the kind of person he was, as much as in the kind of truth he was asked to believe. He seemed naturally to look on the dark side of things. He was the kind of person who looks at the glass and sees that it is half empty instead of half full. We all know the kind of person. Perhaps we are even like Thomas ourselves. Good things always seem too good to be true, and bad things seem to happen all too easily. If like Thomas we have a pessimistic personality, it does little good to pretend that faith comes easily to everyone. Some people find things more difficult than others all along the line.

In Jesus' parable of the ten talents, each servant started out with one talent. Through investment some servants easily turned the one into ten, others turned theirs into five, and some had trouble even earning one. In the end, however, the willingness to risk all for their master was more important than the amount earned. Likewise our willingness to believe the good news of the Resurrection, to hope in God, to change our pessimistic attitude towards life is more important than the mighty miracles of faith that some seem so easily to experience. If we recognise ourselves in Thomas, perhaps we need to examine our pessimistic outlook. Is our failure to believe in God's power really a failure to know ourselves, a personality deficiency that we will not admit?

Faith and Attitudes

A pessimistic temperament is one thing; what one

does with it is another. The first may be constitutional; the second may be controlled. Thomas could not help his pessimistic temperament, but he could have helped his behaviour.

His first mistake was to indulge in solitude. When the other disciples gathered together on the evening of the Resurrection, Thomas was not there. When Jesus appeared to them, turning fear to joy and anxiety to peace, Thomas was not there. Instead he kept to himself. He nursed his sorrow and brooded over his fear. He wouldn't talk to anyone nor discuss the matter with anyone. He didn't hear Jesus say, 'Peace be with you!' because he was not there. 'Let us not give up meeting together, as some are in the habit of doing, but let us encourage one another' (Heb. 10:25). Just as Jesus appeared to the assembled disciples to turn fear to faith, so he promised to appear wherever believers assemble, no matter how dispirited or pessimistic. 'For where two or three come together in my name, there am I with them' (Matt. 18:20).

Thomas's second mistake was to intensify his scepticism by speaking emphatically about it. 'When the other disciples told him that they had seen the Lord, he declared, "Unless I see the nail marks in his hands and put my finger where the nails were, and put my hand into his side, I will not believe it"' (John 20:25). Speech gives staying power to attitudes. We can almost hear him saying, 'I told you that disaster would happen, and now it has. Let's not delude ourselves. The women at the tomb were so overwrought that they just imagined that an angel appeared. You people just had a hallucination last night. You didn't really see Jesus. Things like that just don't happen. It was just wishful thinking. I don't believe it.' The more Thomas talked, the stronger his scepticism became.

Thomas's third mistake was to insist on signs. He demanded tangible, visible evidence. He wanted to see the nailprints and touch the wounds. He demanded evidence, but he didn't really expect to see it. He laid down conditions for his belief that, according to the force of the original language, he thought would never be fulfilled. Unbelief was important to him. Perhaps even then he had earned from his fellow disciples that epithet 'doubting Thomas.' His scepticism had gained for himself a certain notoriety. It was attention-catching. It gave him a certain status in his own eyes, and he didn't want to part with it easily.

Faith and Sight

A week later the disciples again met behind locked doors, and this time Thomas was there. No doubt the other disciples had urged him to be there, and perhaps he had agreed to come as a kind of test. Would Jesus really appear again? Would he dare to meet Thomas's conditions for belief? Whatever the reason, Thomas was there, and suddenly Jesus was there too saying, 'Peace be with you!' 'Then he said to Thomas, "Put your finger here; see my hands. Reach out your hand and put it into my side. Stop doubting and believe"' (John 20:27). Item by item Jesus met his demand. He challenged the sceptic to carry out his test. Faith in the Resurrection was difficult, but not impossible, and Jesus deliberately met Thomas on his own ground, in the midst of his pessimism and scepticism, offering him visual, tangible proof in order to create belief.

The next move was up to Thomas. Could he set aside his pessimism and his scepticism and believe? Or was the pessimistic attitude toward life too ingrained, the scepticism too important to allow faith to work? Others had seen the same evidence and still scoffed. Jesus himself had predicted in the parable of Dives and Lazarus that people would remain unconvinced 'even if someone rises from the dead' (Luke 16:31). There must have been a dramatic moment of silence as faith struggled with doubt inside Thomas. It is not easy in a moment to overturn the habit of a lifetime.

But Thomas passed his test. In one exclamation—'My Lord and my God!'—he moved from pessimism to faith, from scepticism to belief. In the first part of his address to Jesus, he recognised that he who was dead is now alive: 'My Lord, my beloved Master.' The Jesus standing before him was the same Jesus he had loved and followed. He accepted the miraculous fact of the Resurrection. From the fact he then rose to the doctrine. In the second part of his statement, he acknowledged Christ's divinity: 'My God.' Here was his risen Lord and therefore his God, for if death held no power over him, he must be divine. Nor did Thomas make just an intellectual commitment to replace his intellectual scepticism. It was personal. He related his entire response to himself: '*My* Lord and *my* God!'

Thomas's faith came by sight. Perhaps that is why he is there in the Resurrection drama. His scepticism, his insistence on tangible, visual proof of the Resurrection, forever lays to rest the argument that the disciples were credulous and deluded. Frightened as they were, they did not just experience a mass hallucination. When Jesus appeared to them, it was not an illusion but Jesus himself in a resurrected body with nail-prints and wounds that Thomas could see and touch.

In spite of Thomas's test, though, the sceptic in us may still be saying, 'If only I could see, then I would believe.' Perhaps some of us are hiding behind our scepticism, using it as an excuse for doing wrong. Secure in our knowledge that we can't know about the Resurrection for sure, we are unwilling to confront Jesus by faith. In her short story 'A Good Man is Hard to Find,' American writer Flannery O'Connor tells the tale of a grandmother and her family held hostage by an escaped convict, called The Misfit, who uses scepticism as his excuse for doing wrong. While his accomplices lead the members of the family off one by one to be shot, The Misfit engages the grandmother in a theological discussion.

> 'Jesus was the only One that ever raised the dead,' The Misfit said, 'and He shouldn't have done it. He thrown everything off balance. If He did what He said, then it's nothing for you to do but throw away everything and follow Him, and if He didn't, then it's nothing for you to do but enjoy the few minutes you got left the best way you can—by killing somebody or burning down his house or doing some other meanness to him. No pleasure but meanness,' he said and his voice had become almost a snarl.
>
> 'Maybe He didn't raise the dead,' the old

lady mumbled, not knowing what she was saying and feeling so dizzy that she sank down in the ditch with her legs twisted under her.

'I wasn't there so I can't say He didn't,' The Misfit said. 'I wisht I had of been there,' he said, hitting the ground with his fist. 'It ain't right I wasn't there because if I had of been there I would of known. Listen lady,' he said in a high voice, 'if I had of been there I would of known and I wouldn't be like I am now.'

The Misfit, like Thomas, was hiding behind his scepticism, holding out for conditions that he did not expect to be fulfilled. Tangible proof of the resurrected Jesus, however, is not confined to the apostolic age. Whenever good is returned for evil, blessing for cursing, love for hate, Jesus once again shows us the power of his Resurrection in the tangible, visible lives of the people we encounter. In every act of good and kindness and love Jesus shows us the nailprints and wounds of his resurrected body. In the midst of mental torture, murder, and certain death, the grandmother in the story shows The Misfit the tangible evidence he has demanded.

The grandmother's head cleared for an instant. She saw the man's face twisted close to her own as if he were going to cry and she murmured, 'Why, you're one of my babies. You're one of my own children!' She reached out and touched him on the shoulder.

Her gesture of forgiveness and love, like Christ's forgiveness to the soldiers who crucified him, showed The Misfit that he stood in the presence of the resurrected Jesus. He had no excuse now. He couldn't hide behind his scepticism any longer. Like Thomas he had to choose. To use his own words, 'If He did what He said, then it's nothing for you to do but throw away everything and follow Him.' Like the soldiers at the Crucifixion, though, The Misfit does finish the job. Almost by reflex action he kills the grandmother, but his final line in the story—'It's no real pleasure in life.'—shows that he has begun the long road back from evil to good. No longer able to hide behind his scepticism, no longer able to use the excuse that he can't know for sure about the Resurrection of Jesus, The Misfit has taken the first step away from evil toward redemption and faith. In the lives of his saints Christ still confronts the sceptic and offers visible, tangible proof of his Resurrection.

But how much evidence does it take to convince a sceptic? Instead of relying on tangible proof of his Resurrection, Jesus offers us a more excellent way, the way of faith. To Thomas he said, 'Because you have seen me, you have believed; blessed are those who have not seen and yet have believed' (John 20:29). To those first-century Christians who had not seen Jesus either before or after his Resurrection, Peter wrote,

'Praise be to the God and Father of our Lord Jesus Christ! In his great mercy he has given us new birth into a living hope through the resurrection of Jesus Christ from the dead ... Though you have not seen him, you love him; and even though you do not see him now, you believe in him and are filled with an inexpressible and glorious joy, for you are receiving the goal of your faith, the salvation of your souls' (I Peter 1:3, 8, 9).

Faith is not confined to the apostolic age. Faith is possible without sight.

How do we achieve it? John gives the answer: the Word of God. 'Jesus did many other miraculous signs in the presence of his disciples, which are not recorded in this book. But these are written that you may believe that Jesus is the Christ, the Son of God, and that by believing you may have life in his name' (John 20:30, 31). The Word of God creates faith. 'Faith comes from hearing the message, and the message is heard through the word of Christ' (Romans 10:17). Here, then, is the challenge. Faith in the Resurrection is difficult, especially for those like Thomas who have a pessimistic temperament and who are naturally inclined toward scepticism; but Jesus stands ready to meet us, just as he met Thomas, at the point of our pessimism and scepticism. Just as he created faith in the travellers to Emmaus by opening the Scriptures to them, so he stands ready through his Spirit to open his Word to our understanding. It is left for us, like the father who brought his boy to Jesus for healing, to cry, 'I do believe; help me overcome my unbelief!' (Mark 9:24).

CHAPTER 15

ON THE ROAD TO EMMAUS

While the rest of the disciples and followers of Jesus hid behind locked doors in Jerusalem for fear of the Jews (John 20:19), Cleopas and his unnamed companion, the final players in the drama of the Cross, travelled the road down from Jerusalem to Emmaus. They were the only followers of Jesus who made any move out of the city after the Sabbath that followed so closely on the Crucifixion. Either out of necessity or disillusionment, or perhaps just because they preferred to walk instead of remaining indoors, they were on the move on that first day of the week. What kind of people were Cleopas and his companion? What difficulties and doubts did they struggle with? And how did Jesus deal with them?

A Lively Discussion

As they walked the seven-mile journey, 'They were talking with each other about everything that had happened' (Luke 24:14). In the next verse, Luke adds another verb which means 'to debate', or 'to argue'. This word indicates a lively and heated conversation. When Jesus accosts them—'What are you discussing together?' (v 17)—he uses a particular idiomatic expression that means 'What are these words you are putting or placing or throwing against each other?' The word he uses is the one from which we get 'anti-ballistic', and it suggests an image of verbal missiles fired against each other, assertion exploded by rejoinder in mid air between them. A lively discussion indeed.

When Jesus, the stranger, asked them, 'What are you discussing together as you walk along?' they stood still, their faces downcast (Luke 24:17). It was an exasperating interruption of a heated conversation by a totally unbelievable question. They were dumbfounded. Their breath was taken away, and they stopped and stared at him. The short shrift that they gave to the stranger's question further bears out the animation of their talk. 'Are you the only visitor in Jerusalem who doesn't know the things that have been happening there these last few days?' (Luke 24:18, GNB).

We should not get the impression that these two on the road to Emmaus were overcome with gloomy grief, as is sometimes represented. They were eager to talk about and sift the significance of what had happened. Note their lengthy reply (vv 19–24) to Jesus' short question 'What things?' The words come out in a volley: He was a powerful prophet. The chief priests sentenced him to death. They crucified him. That was three days ago. Moreover, now some of our women say that the tomb is empty. They saw an angel who said that he was alive. Some of our friends also went to the tomb but didn't see him.

The short sentences suggest a staccato delivery as they fire their information at the stranger, interrupting each other to add further details. It would almost seem that what had happened in Jerusalem, instead of causing grief, fuelled their powers of conversation. Instead of being afraid or having the centre knocked out of their lives as others in the Resurrection narrative did, they were debating and discussing.

This, then, gives us the character of these two men. They were talkers more than walkers. The important thing in the story is not that they were walking from Jerusalem to Emmaus, but that they were engaged in heated conversation while they went. Some of us are like them. We have a great propensity for talking, a great liking for debate and discussion. There must always be conversation. We all know the kind of person: he must always say something; he must always make you say something; he must talk. Everything issues in conversation. What is the point of anything happening but to be talked about?

The Danger of the Talkative

Jesus replies, 'How foolish you are!' The word he uses signifies a person who has no knowledge or who has imperfect knowledge.

They were not completely ignorant, for when he spoke to them from the Scriptures, they said in retrospect, 'Wasn't it like a fire burning in us when he talked to us on the road and explained the Scriptures to us?' (Luke 24:32, GNB). The kind of person whose heart burns within him as he hears another man unfold the Scriptures is the person who has some knowledge of the Scriptures, who begins to see the things clicking into place. Their response presupposes some familiarity with the subject, but not enough. This is the danger of the talkative person. He often ends up with only a partial grasp. He starts off with a little information and talks about it. The more he talks, the less he listens, and his understanding falls short.

Jesus also called them 'slow of heart to believe'. The person prone to discussion is often slow to believe. The discussion must go on, the nuances must be debated, the implications tested, all the possibilities examined. The classical text on this subject is Paul's two letters to Timothy. He tells Timothy to guard against people who 'only produce arguments; they do not serve God's plan, which is known by faith' (I Tim. 1:4, GNB). He speaks about people who are anxious to engage in 'meaningless talk' (I Tim. 1:6). 'They want to be teachers of the law, but they do not know what they are talking about or what they so confidently affirm' (I Tim. 1:7). They are 'conceited and understand nothing' (I Tim. 6:3), and they have 'an unhealthy interest in controversies and arguments' (I Tim. 6:4). They indulge in 'godless chatter and the opposing ideas of what is falsely called knowledge' (I Tim. 6:20). They 'will not put up with sound doctrine. Instead, to suit their own desires, they will gather around them a great number of teachers to say what their itching ears want to hear. They will turn their ears away from the truth and turn aside to myths' (II Tim. 4:3, 4). When Paul wrote to Timothy, one of the problems in the Church was people who liked to talk and talk and go on talking and never arrive at belief.

Doubt and Disappointment

The two on the road to Emmaus were at least tempted to that doubt because of disappointment—'We had hoped that he would be the one who was going to set

Israel free!' (Luke 24:21, GNB). Here they were wise after the event: this is another characteristic of this kind of person. Perhaps they were not nearly so forthcoming while Jesus was alive. Now that he had gone, however, they could safely say that they 'had hoped'. This tallies with their incredulous reaction to the women's story that the tomb was empty. They were quite satisfied that Jesus was dead and gone.

Could these men even have had an unadmitted sense of relief at what had happened? Were they getting close to involvement and commitment to Jesus Christ? When he died and went into the tomb, they were free to go back home. What had been becoming hot morally and spiritually had suddenly cooled, and they were glad that the pressure was off. This is only a guess, but the kind of guess that would be true about the talkative person facing a decision. That kind of person likes any interruption that will take off the pressure and let him relax and remain uncommitted.

The Age of Discussion

Some people are like that today. This is the age of discussion, of dialogue, of commissions of inquiry, of seminars, of debates. When they have formed a committee to discuss a matter, many people think that they have done something. Sometimes they have; as often they have not. We believe in talk. We have endowed that word 'dialogue' with tremendous significance. Of course, people must talk, but the insidious suggestion that talk alone can solve problems is wrong. Talk cannot do it.

This is the trouble with many people's involvement with Jesus Christ. They talk about him, but will not commit themselves to belief. Scotland after the Second World War was the age of the Youth Fellowships, when the pet word was 'discussion'. America in the sixties and seventies saw the age of 'rap sessions'. Years later little has happened as a result of the discussions. The people who still believe believed before the discussions, and the others simply got tired of the discussions and are not to be found today. How far does our interest in Christianity go? To listening? To talking? Or have we come to the point where we commit ourselves and begin to act?

Proof from the Scriptures

The story does have a touch of ironic humour. What method did Jesus use with these men? He let them talk. His first question was, 'What are you discussing?' They explode, 'Are you the only visitor in Jerusalem who doesn't know the things that have been happening there these last few days?' (Luke 24:18, GNB). Quietly and with some humour, he innocently asks, 'What things?' He is drawing them out, and they rise to the bait, going on one after the other filling in the details. They do not recognise him; they are so engrossed in the conversation that they pay little attention to who he is.

Then he adopts their own approach: argument. 'And Jesus explained to them what was said about himself in all the Scriptures, beginning with the books of Moses and the writings of all the prophets' (Luke 24:27, GNB). He took them up at their point of conversation, and from the Old Testament in passage after passage he showed them how what had happened was what had been prophesied; that there had been a necessity attached to it all; that it was not the end; that it was necessary not only that Christ should suffer but that he should enter into his glory. They were walking seven miles, a lengthy discussion if it can accurately be said that he explained to them 'all the Scriptures'.

Jesus' methods differ according to different people. When he appeared to Mary, there was no mention of the Scriptures. Mary knew all that she needed to know for the time being; he approached her with tenderness, with reassurance. When he appeared to Cleopas and his companion, however, he took the argumentative approach, for their problem was intellectual indecisiveness. With the precision and humour of a skilled debater, Jesus led them to an intellectual decision.

Conviction from Experience

The real conviction, however, did not come while he was talking to them about the Scriptures or arguing with them along their own lines of reasoning. The argument was a necessary prelude, or Jesus would not have taken the pains to discuss with them as he did. He was clearing the ground. He was taking away the difficulties. He was putting Cleopas and his companion into the place where they could become convinced, but in fact the conviction did not come as a result of the argument. It came when they had made a little commitment of themselves. 'As they came near the village to which they were going, Jesus acted as if he were going farther; but they held him back, saying, "Stay with us; the day is almost over and it is getting dark" ' (Luke 24:28, 29, GNB). Their request implied that they were impressed with what he had said and were ready to hear more, and that little shred, that little hair of commitment led to discovery. It came when they sat at table and he broke bread and blessed it and gave it to them. At that moment they recognised Jesus, and in that moment he disappeared. Their real conviction did not come with the argument. It came with the experience.

They had an intuitive experience. They knew! It is always disconcerting to ask someone, 'How do you know?' only to receive the reply 'I know I know.' Yet just that happened to these men. They had argued for seven miles; they came to the table, Jesus broke bread, and in an instant they knew. How did they know? They knew they knew! We call this intuitive knowledge, knowledge that comes with a sudden burst of certainty.

We have two ways to knowledge: cognitive knowledge that comes through information, education, and discussion; and intuitive knowledge that comes through awareness or instinct. How slow life would be if we had only cognitive knowledge, if all we knew had to be learned by rote! Instead, God has given us two valid ways to knowledge. Cleopas and his companion had an existential experience of Christ. In a sudden grasp of intuition they knew Jesus, and in this same way many men come to faith, both in the Bible and out of it.

In our lives intuitive knowledge must balance cognitive knowledge. There has to be an interaction between what we know because we know and what we know because we learn it and reason it out and prove it. We arrive at truth through both of these ways. God has given us both reason and intuition, the one to check the other. God has given us an objective Christian faith, one that has a cognitive part to it, that involves the intellect. That is why we have our reason and the objective truths of the Bible. God has also given us a subjective Christian faith, one that involves experience. The Christian goes forward in his faith with a balance of the two—his subjective experience tested by the Scriptures and his understanding of the Scriptures tested by his experience. Life is warped and crooked unless these two things are balanced. On the road to Emmaus Jesus cleared the ground on the cognitive side by showing to them in all the Scriptures that his body had to be broken, but they came to faith in an intuitive existential experience over the broken bread.

Here is the difficulty with the discussers and the talkers. They concentrate on only one side of these means we have to knowledge. They are ever learning and never coming to a knowledge of the truth, because they think that the whole of life consists in what one can learn, in what one can read in a book. Life does not work like that. A great area of life never comes within that orbit. That is where the discussers and the talkers fall short. They are occupied all the time with evidence, with facts, but do not arrive at the knowledge of the truth because they never commit themselves to experience the truth. God speaks to us through argument and through his Word, and he also has given us the power to know him and experience him. Only as these two balance and harmonise shall we become men of faith in the risen Christ, like the two on the road to Emmaus.